New Mediterranean Diet

Cookbook for Beginners

Perfectly Easy and Amazing Recipes for Living and Lifelong Health with a BONUS 6-Week Meal Plan (Full Color Pictures)

Josie J. Harris

TABLE OF CONTENTS

INTRODUCTION

As a Mediterranean diet recipe author, my journey with Mediterranean cuisine began with a profound appreciation for its rich flavors, wholesome ingredients, and healthful benefits. Growing up, I was exposed to a variety of Mediterranean dishes through family gatherings, where food was always central to our celebrations. The vibrant colors and aromatic spices of dishes like Greek salads, Spanish paellas, and Italian pasta dishes captivated my senses and sparked my curiosity about the culinary traditions of the region.

As I delved deeper into the world of Mediterranean cooking, I discovered the underlying principles that guided this culinary tradition: an emphasis on fresh, seasonal ingredients, a balance of lean proteins, whole grains, and healthy fats, and a focus on simple, yet flavorful preparations. These principles resonated with me not only from a culinary standpoint but also from a perspective of holistic health and well-being.

Inspired by my newfound passion for Mediterranean cuisine, I began experimenting with traditional recipes, putting my own creative twist on classic dishes while staying true to the core principles of the diet. I found that by incorporating more fruits, vegetables, legumes, and olive oil into my meals, I not only enjoyed a greater variety of flavors but also felt more energized and nourished from the inside out.

My passion for the Mediterranean Diet has inspired me to further explore its benefits, including reducing the risk of chronic disease. I hope to inspire others through my recipes to discover the joys of fresh, healthy ingredients while enjoying all the benefits Mediterranean flavours have to offer.

Today, as a Mediterranean diet recipe author, I am committed to spreading awareness about the Mediterranean way of eating and empowering others to embrace this lifestyle for improved health and vitality. Through my recipes, I hope to inspire individuals to discover the joy of cooking with fresh, wholesome ingredients and experience the many benefits of embracing a Mediterranean-inspired diet.

Why Choose The Mediterranean Diet?

The Mediterranean diet offers a flavorful and diverse approach to eating that is deeply rooted in tradition and culture. Its emphasis on fresh, whole foods like fruits, vegetables, whole grains, and healthy fats makes it not only delicious but also incredibly nutritious. With its proven health benefits, including reduced risk of heart disease and other chronic conditions, the Mediterranean diet is a lifestyle choice that promotes longevity and overall well-being.

Health Benefits: The Mediterranean diet is renowned for its numerous health benefits, including reduced risk of heart disease, stroke, and certain cancers. Its emphasis on fresh fruits, vegetables, whole grains, and olive oil contributes to better overall health and longevity.

Balanced and Varied: This diet offers a balanced and varied approach to eating, incorporating a wide range of food groups. It includes plenty of fruits, vegetables, nuts, seeds, legumes, whole grains, and lean proteins, providing essential nutrients and antioxidants.

Rich in Healthy Fats: The Mediterranean diet

Mediterranean countries, where meals are often enjoyed leisurely with family and friends, promoting a sense of community and well-being.

Health Benefits Of The Mediterranean Diet

With its emphasis on fresh, wholesome ingredients and a balanced approach to eating, the Mediterranean diet offers a plethora of health benefits. From reducing the risk of chronic diseases to promoting overall well-being, this dietary pattern has garnered attention for its positive impact on health. Let's explore some of the key health benefits associated with the Mediterranean diet.

Heart Health: The Mediterranean diet is renowned for its ability to promote cardiovascular health. Its emphasis on olive oil, nuts, seeds, and fish rich in omega-3 fatty acids helps lower cholesterol levels, reduce blood pressure, and decrease the risk of heart disease.

Enhanced Brain Function: Research suggests that the Mediterranean diet's combination of antioxidant-rich fruits, vegetables, and omega-3 fatty acids can protect cognitive function and may even lower the risk of neurodegenerative diseases like Alzheimer's.

Weight Management: Unlike restrictive fad diets, the Mediterranean diet encourages a balanced approach to eating, focusing on nutrient-dense foods like fruits, vegetables, whole grains, and lean proteins. This makes it easier to maintain a healthy weight without feeling deprived.

Anti-Inflammatory Effects: Chronic inflammation

promotes the consumption of healthy fats, particularly those found in olive oil, nuts, and fatty fish like salmon and sardines. These fats are beneficial for heart health and help reduce inflammation in the body.

Sustainable and Environmentally Friendly: With its focus on plant-based foods and minimal processed ingredients, the Mediterranean diet is environmentally friendly and sustainable. It encourages the use of locally sourced, seasonal ingredients, supporting local farmers and reducing carbon footprint.

Enjoyable and Flexible: Unlike restrictive fad diets, the Mediterranean diet is enjoyable and flexible, making it easier to maintain long-term. It emphasizes the enjoyment of food, social dining experiences, and moderate indulgence in treats like wine and desserts.

Cultural and Social Aspects: Beyond its nutritional benefits, the Mediterranean diet is deeply rooted in culture and tradition. It reflects the lifestyle of

is linked to various health issues, including heart disease, cancer, and arthritis. By incorporating foods like olive oil, fatty fish, and nuts, the Mediterranean diet helps combat inflammation and promotes overall well-being.

Disease Prevention: Studies have shown that adhering to the Mediterranean diet can reduce the risk of developing chronic conditions such as type 2 diabetes, certain cancers, and metabolic syndrome. Its abundance of fiber, antioxidants, and healthy fats supports optimal health and longevity.

Longevity: Perhaps most notably, the Mediterranean diet is associated with longevity. Its emphasis on fresh, whole foods, coupled with moderate consumption of red wine and regular physical activity, contributes to a longer and healthier life.

The Mediterranean Diet Food Pyramid

The Mediterranean Diet Food Pyramid is a visual representation of the dietary guidelines followed by populations in Mediterranean regions. It illustrates the recommended daily food intake for optimal health and well-being based on traditional Mediterranean eating patterns. Understanding the Mediterranean Diet Food Pyramid can provide valuable insights into the principles and priorities of this renowned dietary approach.

1.Plant-Based Foods: At the base of the Mediterranean Diet Food Pyramid are plant-based foods like fruits, vegetables, whole grains, legumes, nuts, and seeds. These foods provide essential vitamins, minerals, fiber, and antioxidants, promoting overall health and well-being.

2.Olive Oil: Olive oil is a key component of the Mediterranean diet, representing the primary source of fat. Rich in monounsaturated fats and antioxidants, olive oil is used for cooking, salad dressings, and flavoring dishes, contributing to heart health and longevity.

Herbs and Spices: Herbs and spices are used liberally in Mediterranean cuisine to add flavor without the need for excess salt or unhealthy fats. Common herbs and spices include basil, oregano, rosemary, thyme, garlic, and cinnamon, enhancing the taste and nutritional profile of meals.

Fish and Seafood: Fish and seafood are consumed regularly in the Mediterranean diet, providing lean protein, omega-3 fatty acids, and essential nutrients. Fatty fish like salmon, sardines, and mackerel are particularly valued for their heart-healthy benefits.

5.Poultry, Eggs, and Dairy: Poultry, eggs, and dairy products are included in moderation in the Mediterranean diet. Lean cuts of poultry and eggs provide protein and essential nutrients, while dairy products like yogurt and cheese offer calcium and probiotics for bone and gut health.

6.Red Wine (in moderation): Red wine is enjoyed in moderation as part of the Mediterranean diet, typically with meals. Red wine contains antioxidants like resveratrol, which may offer cardiovascular benefits when consumed in moderation and as part of a balanced diet.

Sweets and Desserts (Occasional): Sweets and desserts are consumed occasionally and in small

portions in the Mediterranean diet. Traditional Mediterranean desserts often feature fruits, nuts, honey, and phyllo pastry, offering sweetness and flavor without excessive sugar or unhealthy fats.

8.Red Meat and Processed Foods (Limited): Red meat and processed foods are limited in the Mediterranean diet and consumed sparingly. Instead, emphasis is placed on plant-based sources of protein and healthier alternatives to processed snacks and convenience foods.

Ten Classical Ingredients in Mediterranean Diet

The Mediterranean diet is renowned for its emphasis on fresh, whole foods and vibrant flavors. At the heart of this culinary tradition lie ten classical ingredients that form the cornerstone of Mediterranean cuisine. These ingredients not only contribute to the deliciousness of Mediterranean dishes but also offer numerous health benefits. Let's delve into the essence of these ten classical ingredients and their significance in Mediterranean cooking.

Olive Oil:An essential component of Mediterranean cooking, olive oil serves multiple purposes. It

functions as both a cooking oil and a dressing for salads and vegetables. Additionally, it serves as a flavorful dip for bread.

Tomatoes

Fresh or canned, tomatoes play a vital role in numerous Mediterranean recipes. They are commonly featured in pasta sauces, stews, and salads, adding flavor and depth to these dishes.

3. Garlic

Garlic lends its aromatic essence to a multitude of Mediterranean culinary creations, enhancing the flavors of roasted meats and vegetables, as well as enriching dips and spreads with its distinctive taste.

4. Herbs

Basil, parsley, oregano, and thyme stand among the array of herbs frequently employed in Mediterranean cooking. Renowned for infusing dishes with both flavor and fragrance, they offer versatility, whether utilized fresh or in their dried form.

5. Lemons

Lemons are employed to impart a vibrant and tangy zest to numerous Mediterranean culinary creations, spanning from succulent roasted poultry to delectable seafood dishes.

6. Chickpeas

Chickpeas, a cornerstone of Middle Eastern and Mediterranean culinary traditions, are utilized in crafting iconic dishes such as hummus, falafel, and hearty stews.

Feta cheese

Feta cheese, with its distinctive tanginess and saltiness, is a prevalent component in Greek and Mediterranean cuisine. It finds its way into various dishes, whether crumbled atop salads, incorporated into pasta recipes, or employed as a pizza topping.

8. Eggplant

Eggplant, known for its versatility, lends itself well to roasting, grilling, or frying. It frequently stars in Mediterranean culinary creations like moussaka and baba ghanoush.

9. Couscous

Couscous, a small, grain-like pasta, holds a prominent place in North African and Middle Eastern culinary traditions. It commonly features

as a side dish or serves as a foundation for salads.

10. Yogurt

Yogurt is a prevalent element in Mediterranean cuisine, employed in various capacities such as dips, sauces, and marinades.

Foods To Eat And Avoid

Navigating the Mediterranean diet involves understanding which foods to embrace and which to limit. A balanced approach to food selection is key to reaping the diet's health benefits while savoring its delicious flavors. Let's explore the diverse array of foods to include and avoid to fully embrace the Mediterranean way of eating.

Foods to Eat:

Fresh fruits and vegetables: Embrace a colorful variety of seasonal produce, aiming for at least five servings per day.

Whole grains: Opt for whole grain bread, pasta, rice, and other grains like quinoa and bulgur for fiber and nutrients.

Legumes and nuts: Incorporate beans, lentils, chickpeas, almonds, walnuts, and other nuts for plant-based protein and healthy fats.

Olive oil: Use extra virgin olive oil as your primary source of fat for cooking, dressing, and flavoring dishes.

Fish and seafood: Enjoy fatty fish like salmon, mackerel, and sardines regularly for omega-3 fatty acids.

Poultry and eggs: Choose lean poultry like chicken and turkey, and include eggs as a versatile protein source.

Dairy: Consume moderate amounts of dairy products like Greek yogurt and cheese, preferably low-fat or fat-free varieties.

Herbs and spices: Flavor meals with herbs like basil, oregano, and parsley, and spices like garlic, cumin, and cinnamon for added taste and health benefits.

Foods to Avoid:

Processed meats: Limit intake of processed meats like bacon, sausage, and deli meats due to their high salt and preservative content.

Refined grains: Minimize consumption of refined grains such as white bread, white rice, and sugary cereals in favor of whole grains.

Added sugars: Avoid foods and beverages with added sugars like sugary drinks, candies, and pastries, opting for naturally sweet options instead.

Saturated and trans fats: Limit intake of foods high in saturated and trans fats, such as butter, margarine, and fried foods, to support heart health.

Red meat: Reduce consumption of red meat like beef and lamb, opting for leaner cuts and smaller portions when included.

Processed and fried foods: Steer clear of processed snacks, fast food, and fried foods that are high in unhealthy fats, sodium, and calories.

Refined oils: Minimize the use of refined oils like corn, soybean, and sunflower oil in cooking, favoring olive oil and other healthier options.

Excess salt: Cut back on salt by seasoning foods with herbs, spices, and lemon juice instead of relying on added salt for flavor.

Following the guidelines of the Mediterranean diet, choosing a diverse range of fresh ingredients and healthy fats, while avoiding processed foods and excessive saturated fats and sugars, helps maintain physical and heart health.

1
Breakfasts

Greek Yogurt Parfait with Granola

Prep time: 10 minutes   Cook time: 30 minutes   Serves 4

- For the Granola:
- ¼ cup honey or maple syrup
- 2 tablespoons vegetable oil
- 2 teaspoons vanilla extract
- ½ teaspoon kosher salt
- 3 cups gluten-free rolled oats
- 1 cup mixed raw and unsalted nuts, chopped
- ¼ cup sunflower seeds
- 1 cup unsweetened dried cherries
- For the Parfait:
- 2 cups plain Greek yogurt
- 1 cup fresh fruit, chopped (optional)

1. Preheat the oven to 325ºF (163ºC). Line a baking sheet with parchment paper or foil.
2. Heat the honey, oil, vanilla, and salt in a small saucepan over medium heat. Simmer for 2 minutes and stir together well.
3. In a large bowl, combine the oats, nuts, and seeds. Pour the warm oil mixture over the top and toss well. Spread in a single layer on the prepared baking sheet. Bake for 30 minutes, stirring halfway through.
4. Remove from the oven and add in the dried cherries. Cool completely and store in an airtight container at room temperature for up to 3 months.
5. For one serving: In a bowl or lowball drinking glass, spoon in ½ cup yogurt, ½ cup granola, and ¼ cup fruit (if desired). Layer in whatever pattern you like.

Per Serving:calories: 370 / fat: 144g / protein: 19g / carbs: 44g / fiber: 6g / sodium: 100mg

Summer Day Fruit Salad

Prep time: 5 minutes   Cook time: 0 minutes   Serves 8

- 2 cups cubed honeydew melon
- 2 cups cubed cantaloupe
- 2 cups red seedless grapes
- 1 cup sliced fresh strawberries
- 1 cup fresh blueberries
- Zest and juice of 1 large lime
- ½ cup unsweetened toasted coconut flakes
- ¼ cup honey
- ¼ teaspoon sea salt
- ½ cup extra-virgin olive oil

1. Combine all of the fruits, the lime zest, and the coconut flakes in a large bowl and stir well to blend. Set aside.
2. In a blender, combine the lime juice, honey, and salt and blend on low. Once the honey is incorporated, slowly add the olive oil and blend until opaque.
3. Pour the dressing over the fruit and mix well. Cover and refrigerate for at least 4 hours before serving, stirring a few times to distribute the dressing.

Per Serving:calories: 249 / fat: 15g / protein: 1g / carbs: 30g / fiber: 3g / sodium: 104mg

Tiropita (Greek Cheese Pie)

- 1 tablespoon extra virgin olive oil plus 3 tablespoons for brushing
- 1 pound (454 g) crumbled feta
- 8 ounces (227g) ricotta cheese
- 2 tablespoons chopped fresh mint, or 1 tablespoon dried mint
- 2 tablespoons chopped fresh dill, or 1 tablespoon dried dill
- ¼ teaspoon freshly ground black pepper
- 3 eggs
- 12 phyllo sheets, defrosted
- 1 teaspoon white sesame seeds

1. Preheat the oven to 350°F (180 C). Brush a 9 × 13-inch (23 × 33cm) casserole dish with olive oil.
2. Combine the feta and ricotta in a large bowl, using a fork to mash the ingredients together. Add the mint, dill, and black pepper, and mix well. In a small bowl, beat the eggs and then add them to the cheese mixture along with 1 tablespoon olive oil. Mix well.
3. Carefully place 1 phyllo sheet in the bottom of the prepared dish. (Keep the rest of the dough covered with a damp towel.) Brush the sheet with olive oil, then place a second phyllo sheet on top of the first and brush with olive oil. Repeat until you have 6 layers of phyllo.
4. Spread the cheese mixture evenly over the phyllo and then fold the excess phyllo edges in and over the mixture. Cover the mixture with 6 more phyllo sheets, repeating the process by placing a single phyllo sheet in the pan and brushing it with olive oil. Roll the excess phyllo in to form an edge around the pie.
5. Brush the top phyllo layer with olive oil and then use a sharp knife to score it into 12 pieces, being careful to cut only through the first 3–4 layers of the phyllo dough. Sprinkle the sesame seeds and a bit of water over the top of the pie.
6. Place the pie on the middle rack of the oven. Bake for 40 minutes or until the phyllo turns a deep golden color. Carefully lift one side of the pie to ensure the bottom crust is baked. If it's baked, move the pan to the bottom rack and bake for an additional 5 minutes.
7. Remove the pie from the oven and set aside to cool for 15 minutes. Use a sharp knife to cut the pie into 12 pieces. Store covered in the refrigerator for up to 3 days.

Per Serving:calories: 230 / fat: 15g / protein: 11g / carbs: 13g / fiber: 1g / sodium: 510mg

Peach Sunrise Smoothie

- 1 large unpeeled peach, pitted and sliced (about ½ cup)
- 6 ounces (170 g) vanilla or peach low-fat Greek yogurt
- 2 tablespoons low-fat milk
- 6 to 8 ice cubes

1. Combine all ingredients in a blender and blend until thick and creamy. Serve immediately.

Per Serving:calories: 228 / fat: 3g / protein: 11g / carbs: 42g / fiber: 3g / sodium: 127mg

Quinoa and Yogurt Breakfast Bowls

Prep time: 10 minutes   Cook time: 12 minutes   Serves 8

- 2 cups quinoa, rinsed and drained
- 4 cups water
- 1 teaspoon vanilla extract
- ¼ teaspoon salt
- 2 cups low-fat plain Greek yogurt
- 2 cups blueberries
- 1 cup toasted almonds
- ½ cup pure maple syrup

1. Place quinoa, water, vanilla, and salt in the Instant Pot®. Close lid and set steam release to Sealing. Press the Rice button and set time to 12 minutes.
2. When the timer beeps, let pressure release naturally, about 20 minutes. Open lid and fluff quinoa with a fork.
3. Stir in yogurt. Serve warm, topped with berries, almonds, and maple syrup.

Per Serving:calories: 376 / fat: 13g / protein: 16g / carbs: 52g / fiber: 6g / sodium: 105mg

Lemon–Olive Oil Breakfast Cakes with Berry Syrup

Prep time: 5 minutes   Cook time: 10 minutes   Serves 4

- For the Pancakes:
- 1 cup almond flour
- 1 teaspoon baking powder
- ¼ teaspoon salt
- 6 tablespoon extra-virgin olive oil, divided
- 2 large eggs
- Zest and juice of 1 lemon
- ½ teaspoon almond or vanilla extract
- For the Berry Sauce:
- 1 cup frozen mixed berries
- 1 tablespoon water or lemon juice, plus more if needed
- ½ teaspoon vanilla extract

Make the Pancakes:

1. In a large bowl, combine the almond flour, baking powder, and salt and whisk to break up any clumps.
2. Add the 4 tablespoons olive oil, eggs, lemon zest and juice, and almond extract and whisk to combine well.
3. In a large skillet, heat 1 tablespoon of olive oil and spoon about 2 tablespoons of batter for each of 4 pancakes. Cook until bubbles begin to form, 4 to 5 minutes, and flip. Cook another 2 to 3 minutes on second side. Repeat with remaining 1 tablespoon olive oil and batter. Make the Berry Sauce 1. In a small saucepan, heat the frozen berries, water, and vanilla extract over medium-high for 3 to 4 minutes, until bubbly, adding more water if mixture is too thick. Using the back of a spoon or fork, mash the berries and whisk until smooth.

Per Serving:calories: 381 / fat: 35g / protein: 8g / carbs: 12g / fiber: 4g / sodium: 183mg

Berry Warming Smoothie

Prep time: 5 minutes　　　　　Cook time: 0 minutes　　　　　Serves 1

- ⅔ cup plain kefir or plain yogurt
- ½ cup frozen mixed berries
- ½ cup baby spinach
- ½ cup cucumber, chopped
- 2 tablespoons unsweetened shredded coconut
- ¼ teaspoon grated ginger
- ¼ teaspoon ground cinnamon
- ¼ teaspoon ground nutmeg
- ⅛ teaspoon ground cardamom
- ¼ teaspoon vanilla extract (optional)

1. In a blender or Vitamix, add all the ingredients. Blend to combine.

Per Serving:calories: 165 / fat: 7g / protein: 7g / carbs: 20g / fiber: 4g / sodium: 100mg

Spanish Tortilla with Potatoes and Peppers

- Prep time : 5 minutes / Cook time: 50 minutes / Serves 6

- ½ cup olive oil, plus 2 tablespoons, divided
- 2 pounds (907 g) baking potatoes, peeled and cut into ¼-inch slices
- 2 onions, thinly sliced
- 1 roasted red pepper, drained and cut into strips
- 6 eggs
- 2 teaspoons salt
- 1 teaspoon freshly ground black pepper

1. In a large skillet over medium heat, heat ½ cup of the olive oil. Add the potatoes and cook, stirring occasionally, until the potatoes are tender, about 20 minutes. Remove the potatoes from the pan with a slotted spoon and discard the remaining oil.
2. In a medium skillet over medium heat, heat the remaining 2 tablespoons of olive oil. Add the onions and cook, stirring frequently, until softened and golden brown, about 10 minutes. Remove the onions from the pan with a slotted spoon, leaving the oil in the pan, and add them to the potatoes. Add the pepper slices to the potatoes as well.
3. In a large bowl, whisk together the eggs, salt, and pepper. Add the cooked vegetables to the egg mixture and gently toss to combine.
4. Heat the medium skillet over low heat. Add the egg-vegetable mixture to the pan and cook for about 10 minutes, until the bottom is lightly browned. Use a spatula to loosen the tortilla and transfer the whole thing to a large plate, sliding it out of the pan so that the browned side is on the bottom. Invert the skillet over the tortilla and then lift the plate to flip it back into the skillet with the browned side on top. Return to the stove and continue to cook over low heat until the tortilla is fully set in the center, about 5 more minutes.
5. Serve the tortilla warm or at room temperature.

Per Serving:calories: 370 / fat: 26g / protein: 9g / carbs: 29g / fiber: 5g / sodium: 876mg

Garden Scramble

Prep time: 10 minutes　　　Cook time: 10 minutes　　　Serves 4

- 1 teaspoon extra-virgin olive oil
- ½ cup diced yellow squash
- ½ cup diced green bell pepper
- ¼ cup diced sweet white onion
- 6 cherry tomatoes, halved
- 1 tablespoon chopped fresh basil
- 1 tablespoon chopped fresh parsley
- ½ teaspoon salt
- ¼ teaspoon freshly ground black pepper
- 8 large eggs, beaten

1. In a large nonstick skillet, heat the olive oil over medium heat. Add the squash, pepper, and onion and sauté until the onion is translucent, 3 to 4 minutes.
2. Add the tomatoes, basil, and parsley and season with salt and pepper. Sauté for 1 minute, then pour the beaten eggs over the vegetables. Cover the pan and reduce the heat to low.
3. Cook until the eggs are cooked through, 5 to 6 minutes, making sure that the center is no longer runny.
4. To serve, slide the frittata onto a platter and cut into wedges.

Per Serving:calories: 165 / fat: 11g / protein: 13g / carbs: 3g / fiber: 1g / sodium: 435mg

Greek Breakfast Power Bowl

Prep time: 15 minutes　　　Cook time: 20 minutes　　　Serves 2

- 3 tablespoons extra-virgin avocado oil or ghee, divided
- 1 clove garlic, minced
- 2 teaspoons chopped fresh rosemary
- 1 small eggplant, roughly chopped
- 1 medium zucchini, roughly chopped
- 1 tablespoon fresh lemon juice
- 2 tablespoons chopped mint
- 1 tablespoon chopped fresh oregano
- Salt and black pepper, to taste
- 6 ounces (170 g) Halloumi cheese, cubed or sliced
- ¼ cup pitted Kalamata olives
- 4 large eggs, soft-boiled (or hard-boiled or poached)
- 1 tablespoon extra-virgin olive oil, to drizzle

1. Heat a skillet (with a lid) greased with 2 tablespoons (30 ml) of the avocado oil over medium heat. Add the garlic and rosemary and cook for 1 minute. Add the eggplant, zucchini, and lemon juice. Stir and cover with a lid, then reduce the heat to medium-low. Cook for 10 to 15 minutes, stirring once or twice, until tender.
2. Stir in the mint and oregano. Optionally, reserve some herbs for topping. Season with salt and pepper to taste. Remove from the heat and transfer to a plate. Cover with the skillet lid to keep the veggies warm.
3. Grease the same pan with the remaining 1 tablespoon (15 ml) avocado oil and cook the Halloumi over medium-high heat for 2 to 3 minutes per side until lightly browned. Place the slices of cooked Halloumi on top of the cooked veggies. Top with the olives and cooked eggs and drizzle with the olive oil.
4. Always serve warm, as Halloumi hardens once it cools. Reheat before serving if necessary.

Per Serving:calories: 748 / fat: 56g / protein: 40g / carbs: 25g / fiber: 10g / sodium: 275mg

Jalapeño Popper Egg Cups

Prep time: 10 minutes Cook time: 10 minutes   Serves 2

- 4 large eggs
- ¼ cup chopped pickled jalapeños
- 2 ounces (57 g) full-fat cream cheese
- ½ cup shredded sharp Cheddar cheese

1. In a medium bowl, beat the eggs, then pour into four silicone muffin cups.
2. In a large microwave-safe bowl, place jalapeños, cream cheese, and Cheddar. Microwave for 30 seconds and stir. Take a spoonful, approximately ¼ of the mixture, and place it in the center of one of the egg cups. Repeat with remaining mixture.
3. Place egg cups into the air fryer basket.
4. Adjust the temperature to 320ºF (160ºC) and bake for 10 minutes.
5. Serve warm.

Per Serving:*calories: 375 / fat: 30g / protein: 23g / carbs: 3g / fiber: 0g / sodium: 445mg*

Egg Baked in Avocado

Prep time: 5 minutes   Cook time: 15 minutes   Serves 2

- 1 ripe large avocado
- 2 large eggs
- Salt
- Freshly ground black pepper
- 4 tablespoons jarred pesto, for serving
- 2 tablespoons chopped tomato, for serving
- 2 tablespoons crumbled feta, for serving (optional)

1. Preheat the oven to 425°F(220ºC).
2. Slice the avocado in half and remove the pit. Scoop out about 1 to 2 tablespoons from each half to create a hole large enough to fit an egg. Place the avocado halves on a baking sheet, cut-side up.
3. Crack 1 egg in each avocado half and season with salt and pepper.
4. Bake until the eggs are set and cooked to desired level of doneness, 10 to 15 minutes.
5. Remove from the oven and top each avocado with 2 tablespoons pesto, 1 tablespoon chopped tomato, and 1 tablespoon crumbled feta (if using).

Per Serving:*calories: 248 / fat: 23g / protein: 10g / carbs: 2g / fiber: 1g / sodium: 377mg*

2
Beans and Grains

Sweet Potato and Chickpea Moroccan Stew

Prep time: 10 minutes   Cook time: 40 minutes   Serves 4

- 6 tablespoons extra virgin olive oil
- 2 medium red or white onions, finely chopped
- 6 garlic cloves, minced
- 3 medium carrots (about 8 ounces /227 g), peeled and cubed
- 1 teaspoon ground cumin   • 1 teaspoon ground coriander
- ½ teaspoon smoked paprika
- ½ teaspoon ground turmeric
- 1 cinnamon stick
- ½ pound (227 g) butternut squash, peeled and cut into ½-inch cubes
- 2 medium sweet potatoes, peeled and cut into ½-inch cubes
- 4 ounces (113 g) prunes, pitted
- 4 tomatoes (any variety), chopped, or 20 ounces (567g) canned chopped tomatoes
- 14 ounces (397 g) vegetable broth
- 14 ounces (397 g) canned chickpeas
- ½ cup chopped fresh parsley, for serving

1. Place a deep pan over medium heat and add the olive oil. When the oil is shimmering, add the onions and sauté for 5 minutes, then add the garlic and carrots, and sauté for 1 more minute.
2. Add the cumin, coriander, paprika, turmeric, and cinnamon stick. Continue cooking, stirring continuously, for 1 minute, then add the squash, sweet potatoes, prunes, tomatoes, and vegetable broth. Stir, cover, then reduce the heat to low and simmer for 20 minutes, stirring occasionally and checking the water levels, until the vegetables are cooked through. (If the stew appears to be drying out, add small amounts of hot water until the stew is thick.) 3. Add the chickpeas to the pan, stir, and continue simmering for 10 more minutes, adding more water if necessary. Remove the pan from the heat, discard the cinnamon stick, and set the stew aside to cool for 10 minutes.
4. When ready to serve, sprinkle the chopped parsley over the top of the stew. Store covered in the refrigerator for up to 4 days.

Per Serving:calories: 471 / fat: 23g / protein: 9g / carbs: 63g / fiber: 12g / sodium: 651mg

Earthy Lentil and Rice Pilaf

Prep time: 5 minutes   Cook time: 50 minutes   Serves 6

- ¼ cup extra-virgin olive oil   • 1 large onion, chopped
- 6 cups water   • 1 teaspoon ground cumin
- 1 teaspoon salt   • 1 cup basmati rice
- 2 cups brown lentils, picked over and rinsed

1. In a medium pot over medium heat, cook the olive oil and onions for 7 to 10 minutes until the edges are browned.
2. Turn the heat to high, add the water, cumin, and salt, and bring this mixture to a boil, boiling for about 3 minutes.
3. Add the lentils and turn the heat to medium-low. Cover the pot and cook for 20 minutes, stirring occasionally.
4. Stir in the rice and cover; cook for an additional 20 minutes.
5. Fluff the rice with a fork and serve warm.

Per Serving:calories: 397 / fat: 11g / protein: 18g / carbs: 60g / fiber: 18g / sodium: 396mg

Chickpeas with Spinach and Sun-Dried Tomatoes

Prep time: 10 minutes   Cook time: 2 hours 30 minutes   Serves 3

- ½ pound (227 g) uncooked chickpeas • ¾ teaspoon fine sea salt
- 4 tablespoons extra virgin olive oil, divided
- 2 spring onions (white parts only), sliced
- 1 small onion (any variety), diced
- 1 pound (454 g) fresh spinach, washed and chopped
- ½ cup white wine   • ¼ teaspoon freshly ground black pepper
- ½ cup sun-dried tomatoes (packed in oil), drained, rinsed, and chopped
- 1 tablespoon chopped fresh mint • 1 tablespoon chopped fresh dill
- 6 tablespoons fresh lemon juice, divided

1. Place the chickpeas in a large bowl and cover with cold water by 3 inches (7.5cm) to allow for expansion. Soak overnight or for 12 hours.
2. When ready to cook, drain and rinse the chickpeas. Place them in a large pot and cover with cold water. Place the pot over high heat and bring to a boil (using a slotted spoon to remove any foam), then reduce the heat to low and simmer until the chickpeas are tender but not falling apart, about 1 to 1½ hours, checking the chickpeas every 30 minutes to ensure they aren't overcooking. Use the slotted spoon to transfer the chickpeas a medium bowl and then reserve the cooking water. Set aside.
3. In a deep pan, heat 3 tablespoons of the olive oil over medium heat. When the oil begins to shimmer, add the spring onions and diced onions, and sauté for 5 minutes or until soft, then add the spinach. Toss and continue cooking for 5–7 minutes or until the spinach has wilted. Add the wine and continue cooking for 2 minutes or until the liquid has evaporated.
4. Add the cooked chickpeas, sun-dried tomatoes, mint, dill, 3 tablespoons of the lemon juice, black pepper, and 1½ cups of the chickpea cooking water. Bring the mixture to a boil and then reduce the heat to low and simmer for 30–45 minutes or until the liquid has been absorbed and the chickpeas have thickened, adding more water as needed if the chickpeas appear to be too dry. About 5 minutes before removing the chickpeas from the heat, add the remaining 1 tablespoon of olive oil, a tablespoon of the lemon juice, and the sea salt. Mix well, then remove the pan from the heat, keeping it covered, and set aside to rest for 5 minutes.
5. Divide the mixture between three bowls and top each serving with 1 tablespoon of the lemon juice. Store covered in the refrigerator for up to 3 days.

Per Serving: calories: 599 / fat: 24g / protein: 24g / carbs: 81g / fiber: 17g / sodium: 764mg

Earthy Whole Brown Lentil Dhal

Prep time: 10 minutes   Cook time: 6 to 8 hours   Serves 6

- 6⅓ cups hot water   • 2 cups whole brown lentils
- 1 tablespoon ghee   • 1 teaspoon freshly grated ginger
- 1 teaspoon sea salt   • 1 teaspoon turmeric
- 7 to 8 ounces (198 to 227 g) canned tomatoes
- 4 garlic cloves, finely chopped • 1 onion, chopped
- 1 or 2 fresh green chiles, finely chopped
- 1 teaspoon garam masala   • Handful fresh coriander leaves, chopped

1. Wash and clean the lentils, then set them aside to drain.
2. Heat the slow cooker to high and add all of the ingredients except the garam masala and coriander leaves.
3. Cover and cook on high for 6 hours, or on low for 8 hours.
4. Add the garam masala and fresh coriander leaves before serving, and enjoy.

Per Serving: calories: 263 / fat: 3g / protein: 16g / carbs: 44g / fiber: 8g / sodium: 401mg

Quinoa with Kale, Carrots, and Walnuts

Prep time: 10 minutes   Cook time: 20 minutes   Serves 4

- 1 cup quinoa, rinsed and drained
- 2 cups water
- ¼ cup olive oil
- 2 tablespoons apple cider vinegar
- 1 clove garlic, peeled and minced
- ½ teaspoon ground black pepper
- ½ teaspoon salt
- 2 cups chopped kale
- 1 cup shredded carrot
- 1 cup toasted walnut pieces
- ½ cup crumbled feta cheese

1. Add quinoa and water to the Instant Pot® and stir well. Close lid, set steam release to Sealing, press the Manual button, and set time to 20 minutes. When the timer beeps, let pressure release naturally, about 20 minutes, then open lid. Fluff quinoa with a fork, then transfer to a medium bowl and set aside to cool to room temperature, about 40 minutes.
2. Add oil, vinegar, garlic, pepper, salt, kale, carrot, walnuts, and feta to quinoa and toss well. Refrigerate for 4 hours before serving.

Per Serving:*calories: 625 / fat: 39g / protein: 19g / carbs: 47g / fiber: 10g / sodium: 738mg*

Moroccan Date Pilaf

Prep time: 10 minutes   Cook time: 30 minutes   Serves 4

- 3 tablespoons olive oil
- 1 onion, chopped
- 3 garlic cloves, minced
- 1 cup uncooked long-grain rice
- ½ to 1 tablespoon harissa
- ¼ cup dried cranberries
- 5 or 6 Medjool dates (or another variety), pitted and chopped
- ¼ teaspoon ground cinnamon
- ½ teaspoon ground turmeric
- ¼ teaspoon sea salt
- ¼ teaspoon freshly ground black pepper
- 2 cups chicken broth
- ¼ cup shelled whole pistachios, for garnish

1. In a large stockpot, heat the olive oil over medium heat. Add the onion and garlic and sauté for 3 to 5 minutes, until the onion is soft. Add the rice and cook for 3 minutes, until the grains start to turn opaque. Add the harissa, dates, cranberries, cinnamon, turmeric, salt, and pepper and cook for 30 seconds. Add the broth and bring to a boil, then reduce the heat to low, cover, and simmer for 20 minutes, or until the liquid has been absorbed.
2. Remove the rice from the heat and stir in the nuts. Let stand for 10 minutes before serving.

Per Serving:*calories: 368 / fat: 15g / protein: 6g / carbs: 54g / fiber: 4g / sodium: 83mg*

Falafel

Prep time: 10 minutes   Cook time: 6 to 8 hours   Serves 4

- Nonstick cooking spray
- 2 cups canned reduced-sodium chickpeas, rinsed and drained
- 4 garlic cloves, peeled
- ¼ cup chickpea flour or all-purpose flour
- ¼ cup diced onion
- ¼ cup chopped fresh parsley
- ¼ cup chopped fresh cilantro
- 1 teaspoon sea salt
- 1 teaspoon ground cumin
- ½ teaspoon ground coriander
- ½ teaspoon freshly ground black pepper
- ⅛ teaspoon cayenne pepper

1. Generously coat a slow cooker insert with cooking spray.
2. In a blender or food processor, combine the chickpeas, garlic, flour, onion, parsley, cilantro, salt, cumin, coriander, black pepper, and cayenne pepper. Process until smooth. Form the mixture into 6 to 8 (2-inch) round patties and place them in a single layer in the prepared slow cooker.
3. Cover the cooker and cook for 6 to 8 hours on Low heat.

Per Serving:calories: 174 / fat: 3g / protein: 9g / carbs: 30g / fiber: 8g / sodium: 594mg

Chickpea Fritters

Prep time: 15 minutes   Cook time: 15 minutes   Serves 4

- 3 tablespoons olive oil, plus extra for frying
- 1 onion, chopped
- 2 garlic cloves, minced
- 1 (15-ounce/ 425-g) can chickpeas, drained and rinsed
- 1 teaspoon dried thyme
- 1 teaspoon dried oregano
- 1 teaspoon dried parsley
- Sea salt
- Freshly ground black pepper
- ¾ cup all-purpose flour, plus more as needed

1. In a large skillet, heat 1 tablespoon of the olive oil over medium-high heat. Add the onion and garlic and sauté for 5 to 7 minutes, until the onion is soft. Transfer the onion-garlic mixture to a food processor and add the remaining 2 tablespoons olive oil, the chickpeas, thyme, oregano, and parsley. Season with salt and pepper and purée until a paste forms. (If the mixture is too wet, add 1 to 2 tablespoons of flour and pulse to incorporate.) 2. Place the flour in a bowl. Scoop about 2 tablespoons of the chickpea mixture and roll it into a ball. Dredge the ball in the flour to coat, then flatten the ball slightly and place it on a plate. Repeat with the remaining chickpea mixture.
3. Wipe out the skillet and pour in 2 inches of olive oil. Heat the oil over medium-high heat. Working in batches, fry the fritters in a single layer until golden, about 3 minutes per side. Transfer them to a paper towel–lined plate. Repeat to fry the remaining fritters. Serve immediately.

Per Serving:calories: 290 / fat: 12g / protein: 8g / carbs: 38g / fiber: 6g / sodium: 45mg

3

Beef, Pork, and Lamb

Easy Honey-Garlic Pork Chops

Prep time: 15 minutes　　　　Cook time: 25 minutes　　　　Serves 4

- 4 pork chops, boneless or bone-in
- ¼ teaspoon salt
- ⅛ teaspoon freshly ground black pepper
- 3 tablespoons extra-virgin olive oil
- 5 tablespoons low-sodium chicken broth, divided
- 6 garlic cloves, minced
- ¼ cup honey
- 2 tablespoons apple cider vinegar

1. Season the pork chops with salt and pepper and set aside.
2. In a large sauté pan or skillet, heat the oil over medium-high heat. Add the pork chops and sear for 5 minutes on each side, or until golden brown.
3. Once the searing is complete, move the pork to a dish and reduce the skillet heat from medium-high to medium. Add 3 tablespoons of chicken broth to the pan; this will loosen the bits and flavors from the bottom of the skillet.
4. Once the broth has evaporated, add the garlic to the skillet and cook for 15 to 20 seconds, until fragrant. Add the honey, vinegar, and the remaining 2 tablespoons of broth. Bring the heat back up to medium-high and continue to cook for 3 to 4 minutes.
5. Stir periodically; the sauce is ready once it's thickened slightly. Add the pork chops back into the pan, cover them with the sauce, and cook for 2 minutes. Serve.

Per Serving: *calories: 302 / fat: 16g / protein: 22g / carbs: 19g / fiber: 0g / sodium: 753mg*

Rack of Lamb with Pistachio Crust

Prep time: 10 minutes　　　　Cook time: 19 minutes　　　　Serves 2

- ½ cup finely chopped pistachios
- 3 tablespoons panko bread crumbs
- 1 teaspoon chopped fresh rosemary
- 2 teaspoons chopped fresh oregano
- Salt and freshly ground black pepper, to taste
- 1 tablespoon olive oil
- 1 rack of lamb, bones trimmed of fat and frenched
- 1 tablespoon Dijon mustard

1. Preheat the air fryer to 380ºF (193ºC).
2. Combine the pistachios, bread crumbs, rosemary, oregano, salt and pepper in a small bowl. (This is a good job for your food processor if you have one.) Drizzle in the olive oil and stir to combine.
3. Season the rack of lamb with salt and pepper on all sides and transfer it to the air fryer basket with the fat side facing up. Air fry the lamb for 12 minutes. Remove the lamb from the air fryer and brush the fat side of the lamb rack with the Dijon mustard. Coat the rack with the pistachio mixture, pressing the bread crumbs onto the lamb with your hands and rolling the bottom of the rack in any of the crumbs that fall off.
4. Return the rack of lamb to the air fryer and air fry for another 3 to 7 minutes or until an instant read thermometer reads 140ºF (60ºC) for medium. Add or subtract a couple of minutes for lamb that is more or less well cooked. (Your time will vary depending on how big the rack of lamb is.) 5. Let the lamb rest for at least 5 minutes. Then, slice into chops and serve.

Per Serving: *calories: 716 / fat: 45g / protein: 64g / carbs: 17g / fiber: 5g / sodium: 344mg*

Spaghetti Zoodles and Meatballs

Prep time: 30 minutes   Cook time: 11 to 13 minutes   Serves 6

- 1 pound (454 g) ground beef
- 1½ teaspoons sea salt, plus more for seasoning
- 1 large egg, beaten   • 1 teaspoon gelatin
- ¾ cup Parmesan cheese   • 2 teaspoons minced garlic
- 1 teaspoon Italian seasoning   • Freshly ground black pepper, to taste
- Avocado oil spray   • Keto-friendly marinara sauce, for serving
- 6 ounces (170 g) zucchini noodles, made using a spiralizer or store-bought

1. Place the ground beef in a large bowl, and season with the salt.
2. Place the egg in a separate bowl and sprinkle with the gelatin. Allow to sit for 5 minutes.
3. Stir the gelatin mixture, then pour it over the ground beef. Add the Parmesan, garlic, and Italian seasoning. Season with salt and pepper.
4. Form the mixture into 1½-inch meatballs and place them on a plate; cover with plastic wrap and refrigerate for at least 1 hour or overnight.
5. Spray the meatballs with oil. Set the air fryer to 400ºF (204ºC) and arrange the meatballs in a single layer in the air fryer basket. Air fry for 4 minutes. Flip the meatballs and spray them with more oil. Air fry for 4 minutes more, until an instant-read thermometer reads 160ºF (71ºC). Transfer the meatballs to a plate and allow them to rest.
6. While the meatballs are resting, heat the marinara in a saucepan on the stove over medium heat.
7. Place the zucchini noodles in the air fryer, and cook at 400ºF (204ºC) for 3 to 5 minutes.
8. To serve, place the zucchini noodles in serving bowls. Top with meatballs and warm marinara.

Per Serving: *calories: 176 / fat: 8g / protein: 23g / carbs: 2g / fiber: 0g / sodium: 689mg*

Pork and Cannellini Bean Stew

Prep time: 15 minutes   Cook time: 1 hour   Serves 6

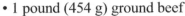

- 1 cup dried cannellini beans
- ¼ cup olive oil
- 1 medium onion, diced
- 2 pounds (907 g) pork roast, cut into 1-inch chunks
- 3 cups water
- 1 (8-ounce/ 227-g) can tomato paste
- ¼ cup flat-leaf parsley, chopped
- ½ teaspoon dried thyme
- Sea salt and freshly ground pepper, to taste

1. Rinse and sort the beans.
2. Cover beans with water, and allow to soak overnight. Heat the olive oil in a large stew pot.
3. Add the onion, stirring occasionally, until golden brown.
4. Add the pork chunks and cook 5 to 8 minutes, stirring frequently, until the pork is browned. Drain and rinse the beans, and add to the pot.
5. Add the water, and bring to a boil. Reduce heat and simmer for 45 minutes, until beans are tender.
6. Add the tomato paste, parsley, and thyme, and simmer for an additional 15 minutes, or until the sauce thickens slightly. Season to taste.

Per Serving: *calories: 373 / fat: 16g / protein: 39g / carbs: 19g / fiber: 4g / sodium: 107mg*

Beef Burger

Prep time: 20 minutes | Cook time: 12 minutes | Serves 4

- 1¼ pounds (567 g) lean ground beef
- 1 tablespoon coconut aminos
- 1 teaspoon Dijon mustard
- A few dashes of liquid smoke
- 1 teaspoon shallot powder
- 1 clove garlic, minced
- ½ teaspoon cumin powder
- ¼ cup scallions, minced
- ⅓ teaspoon sea salt flakes
- ⅓ teaspoon freshly cracked mixed peppercorns
- 1 teaspoon celery seeds
- 1 teaspoon parsley flakes

1. Mix all of the above ingredients in a bowl; knead until everything is well incorporated.
2. Shape the mixture into four patties. Next, make a shallow dip in the center of each patty to prevent them puffing up during air frying.
3. Spritz the patties on all sides using nonstick cooking spray. Cook approximately 12 minutes at 360ºF (182ºC).
4. Check for doneness, an instant-read thermometer should read 160ºF (71ºC). Bon appétit!

Per Serving:calories: 193 / fat: 7g / protein: 31g / carbs: 1g / fiber: 0g / sodium: 304mg

Bulgur and Beef–Stuffed Peppers

Prep time: 15 minutes | Cook time: 26 minutes | Serves 4

- ½ cup bulgur wheat
- 1 cup vegetable broth
- 2 tablespoons olive oil
- 1 medium white onion, peeled and diced
- 1 clove garlic, peeled and minced
- 1 medium Roma tomato, seeded and chopped
- 1 teaspoon minced fresh rosemary
- 1 teaspoon fresh thyme leaves
- ½ teaspoon salt
- ½ teaspoon ground black pepper
- ½ pound (227 g) 90% lean ground beef
- 4 large red bell peppers, tops removed and seeded
- ½ cup marinara sauce
- 1 cup water
- ½ cup grated Parmesan cheese

1. Add bulgur and broth to the Instant Pot® and stir well. Close lid, set steam release to Sealing, press the Rice button, adjust pressure to Low, and set time to 12 minutes. When the timer beeps, quick-release the pressure until the float valve drops. Open lid and fluff bulgur with a fork, then transfer to a medium bowl and set aside to cool.
2. Press the Sauté button and heat oil. Add onion and cook until tender, about 5 minutes. Add garlic, tomato, rosemary, thyme, salt, and pepper. Cook until garlic and herbs are fragrant, about 1 minute.
3. Add ground beef and cook, crumbling well, until no longer pink, about 5 minutes. Press the Cancel button.
4. Add beef mixture to bulgur and mix well. Divide mixture between bell peppers, making sure not to compact the mixture too much. Top each pepper with marinara sauce.
5. Clean out pot, add water, and place rack in pot. Carefully stand peppers on rack. Close lid, set steam release to Sealing, press the Manual button, and set time to 3 minutes. When the timer beeps, quick-release the pressure until the float valve drops. Open lid and carefully transfer peppers with tongs to plates. Top with cheese and serve immediately.

Per Serving:calories: 363 / fat: 17g / protein: 21g / carbs: 31g / fiber: 7g / sodium: 594mg

Filipino Crispy Pork Belly

Prep time: 20 minutes   Cook time: 30 minutes   Serves 4

- 1 pound (454 g) pork belly
- 6 garlic cloves
- 1 teaspoon kosher salt
- 2 bay leaves
- 3 cups water
- 2 tablespoons soy sauce
- 1 teaspoon black pepper

1. Cut the pork belly into three thick chunks so it will cook more evenly.
2. Place the pork, water, garlic, soy sauce, salt, pepper, and bay leaves in the inner pot of an Instant Pot or other electric pressure cooker. Seal and cook at high pressure for 15 minutes. Let the pressure release naturally for 10 minutes, then manually release the remaining pressure. (If you do not have a pressure cooker, place all the ingredients in a large saucepan. Cover and cook over low heat until a knife can be easily inserted into the skin side of pork belly, about 1 hour.) Using tongs, very carefully transfer the meat to a wire rack over a rimmed baking sheet to drain and dry for 10 minutes.
3. Cut each chunk of pork belly into two long slices. Arrange the slices in the air fryer basket. Set the air fryer to 400°F (204°C) for 15 minutes, or until the fat has crisped.
4. Serve immediately.

Per Serving:*calories: 619 / fat: 62g / protein: 12g / carbs: 4g / fiber: 0g / sodium: 743mg*

Cube Steak Roll-Ups

Prep time: 30 minutes   Cook time: 8 to 10 minutes   Serves 4

- 4 cube steaks (6 ounces / 170 g each)
- 1 (16-ounce / 454-g) bottle Italian dressing
- 1 teaspoon salt
- ½ teaspoon freshly ground black pepper
- ½ cup finely chopped yellow onion
- ½ cup finely chopped green bell pepper
- ½ cup finely chopped mushrooms
- 1 to 2 tablespoons oil

1. In a large resealable bag or airtight storage container, combine the steaks and Italian dressing. Seal the bag and refrigerate to marinate for 2 hours.
2. Remove the steaks from the marinade and place them on a cutting board. Discard the marinade. Evenly season the steaks with salt and pepper.
3. In a small bowl, stir together the onion, bell pepper, and mushrooms. Sprinkle the onion mixture evenly over the steaks.

Roll up the steaks, jelly roll-style, and secure with toothpicks.
4. Preheat the air fryer to 400°F (204°C).
5. Place the steaks in the air fryer basket.
6. Cook for 4 minutes. Flip the steaks and spritz them with oil. Cook for 4 to 6 minutes more until the internal temperature reaches 145°F (63°C). Let rest for 5 minutes before serving.

Per Serving:*calories: 364 / fat: 20g / protein: 37g / carbs: 7g / fiber: 1g / sodium: 715mg*

Mustard Lamb Chops

Prep time: 5 minutes   Cook time: 14 minutes   Serves 4

- Oil, for spraying
- 2 teaspoons lemon juice
- ¼ teaspoon salt
- ¼ teaspoon freshly ground black pepper
- 4 (1¼-inch-thick) loin lamb chops
- 1 tablespoon Dijon mustard
- ½ teaspoon dried tarragon

1. Preheat the air fryer to 390ºF (199ºC). Line the air fryer basket with parchment and spray lightly with oil.
2. In a small bowl, mix together the mustard, lemon juice, tarragon, salt, and black pepper.
3. Pat dry the lamb chops with a paper towel. Brush the chops on both sides with the mustard mixture.
4. Place the chops in the prepared basket. You may need to work in batches, depending on the size of your air fryer.
5. Cook for 8 minutes, flip, and cook for another 6 minutes, or until the internal temperature reaches 125ºF (52ºC) for rare, 145ºF (63ºC) for medium-rare, or 155ºF (68ºC) for medium.

Per Serving:calories: 96 / fat: 4g / protein: 14g / carbs: 0g / fiber: 0g / sodium: 233mg

Ground Beef Taco Rolls

Prep time: 20 minutes   Cook time: 10 minutes   Serves 4

- ½ pound (227 g) ground beef
- 1 tablespoon chili powder
- ½ teaspoon garlic powder
- ¼ cup canned diced tomatoes and chiles, drained
- 2 tablespoons chopped cilantro
- 1½ cups shredded Mozzarella cheese
- ½ cup blanched finely ground almond flour
- 2 ounces (57 g) full-fat cream cheese
- ⅓ cup water
- 2 teaspoons cumin
- ¼ teaspoon dried oregano
- 1 large egg

1. In a medium skillet over medium heat, brown the ground beef about 7 to 10 minutes. When meat is fully cooked, drain.
2. Add water to skillet and stir in chili powder, cumin, garlic powder, oregano, and tomatoes with chiles. Add cilantro. Bring to a boil, then reduce heat to simmer for 3 minutes.
3. In a large microwave-safe bowl, place Mozzarella, almond flour, cream cheese, and egg. Microwave for 1 minute. Stir the mixture quickly until smooth ball of dough forms.
4. Cut a piece of parchment for your work surface. Press the dough into a large rectangle on the parchment, wetting your hands to prevent the dough from sticking as necessary. Cut the dough into eight rectangles.
5. On each rectangle place a few spoons of the meat mixture. Fold the short ends of each roll toward the center and roll the length as you would a burrito.
6. Cut a piece of parchment to fit your air fryer basket. Place taco rolls onto the parchment and place into the air fryer basket.
7. Adjust the temperature to 360ºF (182ºC) and air fry for 10 minutes.
8. Flip halfway through the cooking time.
9. Allow to cool 10 minutes before serving.

Per Serving:calories: 411 / fat: 31g / protein: 27g / carbs: 7g / fiber: 3g / sodium: 176mg

Greek Lamb Burgers

Prep time: 10 minutes   Cook time: 10 minutes   Serves 4

- 1 pound (454 g) ground lamb
- ½ teaspoon salt
- ½ teaspoon freshly ground black pepper
- 4 tablespoons feta cheese, crumbled
- Buns, toppings, and tzatziki, for serving (optional)

1. Preheat a grill, grill pan, or lightly oiled skillet to high heat.
2. In a large bowl, using your hands, combine the lamb with the salt and pepper.
3. Divide the meat into 4 portions. Divide each portion in half to make a top and a bottom. Flatten each half into a 3-inch circle. Make a dent in the center of one of the halves and place 1 tablespoon of the feta cheese in the center. Place the second half of the patty on top of the feta cheese and press down to close the 2 halves together, making it resemble a round burger.
4. Cook the stuffed patty for 3 minutes on each side, for medium-well. Serve on a bun with your favorite toppings and tzatziki sauce, if desired.

Per Serving:calories: 345 / fat: 29g / protein: 20g / carbs: 1g / fiber: 0g / sodium: 462mg

Hearty Stewed Beef in Tomato Sauce

Prep time: 20 minutes   Cook time: 1 hour 45 minutes   Serves 5

- 3 tablespoons extra virgin olive oil
- 2 pounds (907 g) boneless beef chuck, cut into 2-inch (5cm) chunks
- 1 medium onion (any variety), diced
- 4 garlic cloves, minced
- ⅓ cup white wine
- 2 tablespoons tomato paste
- 1 cinnamon stick
- 4 cloves
- 4 allspice berries
- 1 bay leaf
- ¼ teaspoon freshly ground black pepper
- 15 ounces (425 g) canned crushed tomatoes or chopped fresh tomatoes
- 1 cup hot water
- ½ teaspoon fine sea salt

1. Add the olive oil to a deep pan over medium heat. When the oil starts to shimmer, place half the beef in the pan. Brown the meat until a crust develops, about 3–4 minutes per side, then transfer the meat to a plate, and set aside. Repeat with the remaining pieces.
2. Add the onions to the pan and sauté for 3 minutes or until soft, using a wooden spatula to scrape the browned bits from the bottom of the pan. Add the garlic and sauté for 1 minute, then add the wine and deglaze the pan for 1 more minute, again using the wooden spatula to scrape any browned bits from the bottom of the pan.
3. Add the tomato paste to the pan while stirring rapidly, then add the cinnamon stick, cloves, allspice berries, bay leaf, black pepper, crushed tomatoes, and hot water. Mix well.
4. Add the beef back to the pan. Stir, then cover and reduce the heat to low. Simmer for 1 hour 30 minutes or until the beef is cooked through and tender, and the sauce has thickened. (If the sauce becomes too dry, add more hot water as needed.) 5. About 10 minutes before the cooking time is complete, add the sea salt and stir. When ready to serve, remove the cinnamon stick, bay leaf, allspice berries, and cloves. Store in the refrigerator for up to 3 days.

Per Serving:calories: 357 / fat: 19g / protein: 39g / carbs: 8g / fiber: 2g / sodium: 403mg

4

Poultry

Herb–Marinated Chicken Breasts

Prep time: 10 minutes   Cook time: 10 minutes   Serves 4

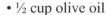

- ½ cup fresh lemon juice
- ¼ cup extra-virgin olive oil
- 4 cloves garlic, minced
- 2 tablespoons chopped fresh basil
- 1 tablespoon chopped fresh oregano
- 1 tablespoon chopped fresh mint
- 2 pounds (907 g) chicken breast tenders
- ½ teaspoon unrefined sea salt or salt
- ¼ teaspoon freshly ground black pepper

1. In a small bowl, whisk the lemon juice, olive oil, garlic, basil, oregano, and mint well to combine. Place the chicken breasts in a large shallow bowl or glass baking pan, and pour dressing over the top.
2. Cover, place in the refrigerator, and allow to marinate for 1 to 2 hours. Remove from the refrigerator, and season with salt and pepper.
3. Heat a large, wide skillet over medium-high heat. Using tongs, place chicken tenders evenly in the bottom of the skillet. Pour the remaining marinade over the chicken.
4. Allow to cook for 3 to 5 minutes each side, or until chicken is golden, juices have been absorbed, and meat is cooked to an internal temperature of 160°F (71°C).

Per Serving: calories: 521 / fat: 35g / protein: 48g / carbs: 3g / fiber: 0g / sodium: 435mg

Lebanese Grilled Chicken

Prep time: 10 minutes   Cook time: 14 minutes   Serves 4

- ½ cup olive oil
- ¼ cup apple cider vinegar
- Zest and juice of 1 lemon
- 4 cloves garlic, minced
- 1 teaspoon sea salt
- 1 teaspoon Arabic 7 spices (baharaat)
- ½ teaspoon cinnamon
- 1 chicken, cut into 8 pieces

1. Combine all the ingredients except the chicken in a shallow dish or plastic bag.
2. Place the chicken in the bag or dish and marinate overnight, or at least for several hours.
3. Drain, reserving the marinade. Heat the grill to medium-high.
4. Cook the chicken pieces for 10–14 minutes, brushing them with the marinade every 5 minutes or so.
5. The chicken is done when the crust is golden brown and an instant-read thermometer reads 180ºF (82ºC) in the thickest parts. Remove skin before eating.

Per Serving: calories: 518 / fat: 34g / protein: 49g / carbs: 4g / fiber: 0g / sodium: 613mg

Chicken and Grape Tomatoes

Prep time: 15 minutes   Cook time: 8 hours   Serves 2

- 1 pint grape tomatoes
- Zest of 1 lemon
- 1 teaspoon extra-virgin olive oil
- 2 bone-in, skinless chicken thighs, about 8 ounces (227 g) each
- 1 teaspoon fresh thyme
- ½ teaspoon fresh rosemary
- ⅛ teaspoon sea salt
- Freshly ground black pepper
- 4 garlic cloves, smashed

1. Put the tomatoes, garlic, lemon zest, and olive oil in the slow cooker. Gently stir to mix.
2. Place the chicken thighs over the tomato mixture and season them with the thyme, rosemary, salt, and a few grinds of black pepper.
3. Cover and cook on low for 8 hours.

Per Serving: calories: 284 / fat: 10g / protein: 40g / carbs: 9g / fiber: 2g / sodium: 366mg

Chicken with Lemon Asparagus

Prep time: 10 minutes   Cook time: 13 minutes   Serves 4

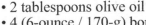

- 2 tablespoons olive oil
- 4 (6-ounce / 170-g) boneless, skinless chicken breasts
- ½ teaspoon ground black pepper
- ¼ teaspoon salt
- ¼ teaspoon smoked paprika
- 2 cloves garlic, peeled and minced
- 2 sprigs thyme
- 2 sprigs oregano
- 1 tablespoon grated lemon zest
- ¼ cup lemon juice
- ¼ cup low-sodium chicken broth
- 1 bunch asparagus, trimmed
- ¼ cup chopped fresh parsley
- 4 lemon wedges

1. Press Sauté on the Instant Pot® and heat oil. Season chicken with pepper, salt, and smoked paprika. Brown chicken on both sides, about 4 minutes per side. Add garlic, thyme, oregano, lemon zest, lemon juice, and chicken broth. Press the Cancel button.
2. Close lid, set steam release to Sealing, press the Manual button, and set time to 5 minutes.
3. When the timer beeps, quick-release the pressure until the float valve drops. Press the Cancel button and open lid. Transfer chicken breasts to a serving platter. Tent with foil to keep warm.
4. Add asparagus to the Instant Pot®. Close lid, set steam release to Sealing, press the Manual button, and set time to 0. When the timer beeps, quick-release the pressure until the float valve drops. Open lid and remove asparagus. Arrange asparagus around chicken and garnish with parsley and lemon wedges. Serve immediately.

Per Serving: calories: 227 / fat: 11g / protein: 35g / carbs: 0g / fiber: 0g / sodium: 426mg

Chicken Cacciatore

Prep time: 20 minutes   Cook time: 1 hour 10 minutes   Serves 4 to6

- 2 tablespoons extra-virgin olive oil   • ½ cup diced carrots
- 2 garlic cloves, minced   • ½ cup chopped celery
- 2 onions, chopped   • 2 pounds (907 g) chicken tenders
- 2 (14½-ounce / 411-g) cans Italian seasoned diced tomatoes, drained
- 2 cups cooked corkscrew pasta, such as whole-grain fusilli

1. In a large saucepan, heat the oil over medium-high heat and sauté the carrots, garlic, celery, and onions for about 5 minutes, until softened. Add the chicken and brown for 4 to 5 minutes on each side.
2. Add the diced tomatoes. Cover and reduce heat to simmer for an hour. Serve over pasta.

Per Serving:calories: 416 / fat: 3g / protein: 58g / carbs: 38g / fiber: 7g / sodium: 159mg

Personal Cauliflower Pizzas

Prep time: 10 minutes   Cook time: 25 minutes   Serves 2

- 1 (12-ounce / 340-g) bag frozen riced cauliflower
- ⅓ cup shredded Mozzarella cheese   • ¼ cup almond flour
- ¼ grated Parmesan cheese   • 1 large egg
- ½ teaspoon salt   • 1 teaspoon garlic powder
- 1 teaspoon dried oregano   • ¼ cup fresh baby arugula, divided
- 4 tablespoons no-sugar-added marinara sauce, divided
- 4 ounces (113 g) fresh Mozzarella, chopped, divided
- 1 cup cooked chicken breast, chopped, divided
- ½ cup chopped cherry tomatoes, divided

1. Preheat the air fryer to 400ºF (204ºC). Cut 4 sheets of parchment paper to fit the basket of the air fryer. Brush with olive oil and set aside.
2. In a large glass bowl, microwave the cauliflower according to package directions. Place the cauliflower on a clean towel, draw up the sides, and squeeze tightly over a sink to remove the excess moisture. Return the cauliflower to the bowl and add the shredded Mozzarella along with the almond flour, Parmesan, egg, salt, garlic powder, and oregano. Stir until thoroughly combined.
3. Divide the dough into two equal portions. Place one piece of dough on the prepared parchment paper and pat gently into a thin, flat disk 7 to 8 inches in diameter. Air fry for 15 minutes until the crust begins to brown. Let cool for 5 minutes.
4. Transfer the parchment paper with the crust on top to a baking sheet. Place a second sheet of parchment paper over the crust. While holding the edges of both sheets together, carefully lift the crust off the baking sheet, flip it, and place it back in the air fryer basket. The new sheet of parchment paper is now on the bottom. Remove the top piece of paper and air fry the crust for another 15 minutes until the top begins to brown. Remove the basket from the air fryer.
5. Spread 2 tablespoons of the marinara sauce on top of the crust, followed by half the fresh Mozzarella, chicken, cherry tomatoes, and arugula. Air fry for 5 to 10 minutes longer, until the cheese is melted and beginning to brown. Remove the pizza from the oven and let it sit for 10 minutes before serving. Repeat with the remaining ingredients to make a second pizza.

Per Serving:calories: 655 / fat: 35g / protein: 67g / carbs: 20g / fiber: 7g / sodium: 741mg

Grape Chicken Panzanella

Prep time: 10 minutes　　　　Cook time: 5 minutes　　　　Serves: 6

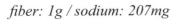

- 3 cups day-old bread (like a baguette, crusty Italian bread, or whole-grain bread), cut into 1-inch cubes
- 5 tablespoons extra-virgin olive oil, divided
- 2 cups chopped cooked chicken breast (about 1 pound / 454 g)
- 1 cup red seedless grapes, halved
- ½ pint grape or cherry tomatoes, halved (about ¾ cup)
- ½ cup Gorgonzola cheese crumbles (about 2 ounces / 57 g)
- ⅓ cup chopped walnuts
- ¼ cup diced red onion (about ⅛ onion)
- 3 tablespoons chopped fresh mint leaves
- ¼ teaspoon freshly ground black pepper
- 1 tablespoon balsamic vinegar
- Zest and juice of 1 small lemon
- 1 teaspoon honey

1. Line a large, rimmed baking sheet with aluminum foil. Set aside. Set one oven rack about 4 inches below the broiler element. Preheat the broiler to high.
2. In a large serving bowl, drizzle the cubed bread with 2 tablespoons of oil, and mix gently with your hands to coat. Spread the mixture over the prepared baking sheet. Place the baking sheet under the broiler for 2 minutes. Stir the bread, then broil for another 30 to 60 seconds, watching carefully so the bread pieces are toasted and not burned. Remove from the oven and set aside.
3. In the same (now empty) large serving bowl, mix together the chicken, grapes, tomatoes, Gorgonzola, walnuts, onion, mint, and pepper. Add the toasted bread pieces, and gently mix together.
4. In a small bowl, whisk together the remaining 3 tablespoons of oil, vinegar, zest and juice from the lemon, and honey. Drizzle the dressing over the salad, toss gently to mix, and serve.

Per Serving:calories: 334 / fat: 21g / protein: 19g / carbs: 19g / fiber: 2g / sodium: 248mg

Blackened Cajun Chicken Tenders

Prep time: 10 minutes　　　　Cook time: 17 minutes　　　　Serves 4

- 2 teaspoons paprika
- 1 teaspoon chili powder
- ½ teaspoon garlic powder
- ½ teaspoon dried thyme
- ¼ teaspoon onion powder
- ⅛ teaspoon ground cayenne pepper
- 2 tablespoons coconut oil
- 1 pound (454 g) boneless, skinless chicken tenders
- ¼ cup full-fat ranch dressing

1. In a small bowl, combine all seasonings.
2. Drizzle oil over chicken tenders and then generously coat each tender in the spice mixture. Place tenders into the air fryer basket.
3. Adjust the temperature to 375°F (191°C) and air fry for 17 minutes.
4. Tenders will be 165°F (74°C) internally when fully cooked. Serve with ranch dressing for dipping.

Per Serving:calories: 266 / fat: 17g / protein: 26g / carbs: 2g / fiber: 1g / sodium: 207mg

Skillet Greek Turkey and Rice

Prep time: 20 minutes   Cook time: 30 minutes   Serves 2

- 1 tablespoon olive oil
- ½ medium onion, minced
- 2 garlic cloves, minced
- 8 ounces (227 g) ground turkey breast
- ½ cup roasted red peppers, chopped (about 2 jarred peppers)
- ¼ cup sun-dried tomatoes, minced
- 1 teaspoon dried oregano
- ½ cup brown rice
- 1¼ cups low-sodium chicken stock
- Salt
- 2 cups lightly packed baby spinach

1. Heat the olive oil in a sauté pan over medium heat. Add the onion and sauté for 5 minutes. Add the garlic and cook for another 30 seconds.
2. Add the turkey breast and cook for 7 minutes, breaking the turkey up with a spoon, until no longer pink.
3. Add the roasted red peppers, sun-dried tomatoes, and oregano and stir to combine. Add the rice and chicken stock and bring the mixture to a boil.
4. Cover the pan and reduce the heat to medium-low. Simmer for 30 minutes, or until the rice is cooked and tender. Season with salt.
5. Add the spinach to the pan and stir until it wilts slightly.

Per Serving:calories: 446 / fat: 17g / protein: 30g / carbs: 49g / fiber: 5g / sodium: 663mg

Mediterranean Roasted Turkey Breast

Prep time: 15 minutes   Cook time: 6 to 8 hours   Serves 4

- 3 garlic cloves, minced
- 1 teaspoon dried oregano
- ½ teaspoon freshly ground black pepper
- ½ teaspoon dried basil
- ½ teaspoon dried rosemary
- ¼ teaspoon dried dill
- 2 tablespoons extra-virgin olive oil
- 2 tablespoons freshly squeezed lemon juice
- 1 (4- to 6-pound / 1.8- to 2.7-kg) boneless or bone-in turkey breast
- 1 teaspoon sea salt
- ½ teaspoon dried parsley
- ½ teaspoon dried thyme
- ¼ teaspoon ground nutmeg

- 1 onion, chopped
- 4 ounces (113 g) whole Kalamata olives, pitted
- 1 cup sun-dried tomatoes (packaged, not packed in oil), chopped
- ½ cup low-sodium chicken broth

1. In a small bowl, stir together the garlic, salt, oregano, pepper, basil, parsley, rosemary, thyme, dill, and nutmeg.
2. Drizzle the olive oil and lemon juice all over the turkey breast and generously season it with the garlic-spice mix.
3. In a slow cooker, combine the onion and chicken broth. Place the seasoned turkey breast on top of the onion. Top the turkey with the olives and sun-dried tomatoes.
4. Cover the cooker and cook for 6 to 8 hours on Low heat.
5. Slice or shred the turkey for serving.

Per Serving:calories: 676 / fat: 19g / protein: 111g / carbs: 14g / fiber: 3g / sodium: 626mg

Niçoise Chicken

Prep time: 20 minutes   Cook time: 50 minutes   Serves 6

- ¼ cup olive oil
- 3 medium onions, coarsely chopped
- 3 cloves garlic, minced
- 4 pounds (1.8 kg) chicken breast from 1 cut-up chicken
- 5 Roma tomatoes, peeled and chopped
- ½ cup white wine
- 1 (14½-ounce / 411-g) can chicken broth
- ½ cup black Niçoise olives, pitted
- Juice of 1 lemon
- ¼ cup flat-leaf parsley, chopped
- 1 tablespoon fresh tarragon leaves, chopped
- Sea salt and freshly ground pepper, to taste

1. Heat the olive oil in a deep saucepan or stew pot over medium heat. Cook the onions and garlic 5 minutes, or until tender and translucent.
2. Add the chicken and cook an additional 5 minutes to brown slightly.
3. Add the tomatoes, white wine, and chicken broth, cover, and simmer 30–45 minutes on medium-low heat, or until the chicken is tender and the sauce is thickened slightly.
4. Remove the lid and add the olives and lemon juice.
5. Cook an additional 10–15 minutes to thicken the sauce further.
6. Stir in the parsley and tarragon, and season to taste. Serve immediately with noodles or potatoes and a dark leafy salad.

Per Serving: *calories: 501 / fat: 15g / protein: 74g / carbs: 11g / fiber: 2g / sodium: 451mg*

Pecan Turkey Cutlets

Prep time: 10 minutes   Cook time: 10 to 12 minutes per batch   Serves 4

- ¾ cup panko bread crumbs
- ¼ teaspoon pepper
- ¼ teaspoon poultry seasoning
- ¼ cup cornstarch
- 1 pound (454 g) turkey cutlets, ½-inch thick
- Salt and pepper, to taste
- ¼ teaspoon salt
- ¼ teaspoon dry mustard
- ½ cup pecans
- 1 egg, beaten
- Oil for misting or cooking spray

1. Place the panko crumbs, ¼ teaspoon salt, ¼ teaspoon pepper, mustard, and poultry seasoning in food processor. Process until crumbs are finely crushed. Add pecans and process in short pulses just until nuts are finely chopped. Go easy so you don't overdo it!
2. Preheat the air fryer to 360ºF (182ºC).
3. Place cornstarch in one shallow dish and beaten egg in another. Transfer coating mixture from food processor into a third shallow dish.
4. Sprinkle turkey cutlets with salt and pepper to taste.
5. Dip cutlets in cornstarch and shake off excess. Then dip in beaten egg and roll in crumbs, pressing to coat well. Spray both sides with oil or cooking spray.
6. Place 2 cutlets in air fryer basket in a single layer and cook for 10 to 12 minutes or until juices run clear.
7. Repeat step 6 to cook remaining cutlets.

Per Serving: *calories: 340 / fat: 13g / protein: 31g / carbs: 24g / fiber: 4g / sodium: 447mg*

5

Fish and Seafood

Fish Tagine

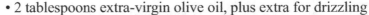

- 2 tablespoons extra-virgin olive oil, plus extra for drizzling
- 1 large onion, halved and sliced ¼ inch thick
- 1 pound (454 g) carrots, peeled, halved lengthwise, and sliced ¼ inch thick
- 2 (2-inch) strips orange zest, plus 1 teaspoon grated zest
- ¾ teaspoon table salt, divided   • 2 tablespoons tomato paste
- 4 garlic cloves, minced, divided
- 1¼ teaspoons paprika
- 1 teaspoon ground cumin
- ¼ teaspoon red pepper flakes
- ¼ teaspoon saffron threads, crumbled
- 1 (8-ounce / 227-g) bottle clam juice
- 1½ pounds (680 g) skinless halibut fillets, 1½ inches thick, cut into 2-inch pieces
- ¼ cup pitted oil-cured black olives, quartered
- 2 tablespoons chopped fresh parsley
- 1 teaspoon sherry vinegar

1. Using highest sauté function, heat oil in Instant Pot until shimmering. Add onion, carrots, orange zest strips, and ¼ teaspoon salt, and cook until vegetables are softened and lightly browned, 10 to 12 minutes. Stir in tomato paste, three-quarters of garlic, paprika, cumin, pepper flakes, and saffron and cook until fragrant, about 30 seconds. Stir in clam juice, scraping up any browned bits.
2. Sprinkle halibut with remaining ½ teaspoon salt. Nestle halibut into onion mixture and spoon some of cooking liquid on top of pieces. Lock lid in place and close pressure release valve. Select high pressure cook function and set cook time for 0 minutes. Once Instant Pot has reached pressure, immediately turn off pot and quick-release pressure.
3. Discard orange zest. Gently stir in olives, parsley, vinegar, grated orange zest, and remaining garlic. Season with salt and pepper to taste. Drizzle extra oil over individual portions before serving.

Per Serving: *calories: 310 / fat: 15g / protein: 34g / carbs: 18g / fiber: 4g / sodium: 820mg*

Almond-Crusted Salmon

- ¼ cup olive oil   • 1 tablespoon honey
- ¼ cup breadcrumbs   • ½ teaspoon dried thyme
- ½ cup finely chopped almonds, lightly toasted
- Sea salt and freshly ground pepper, to taste
- 4 salmon steaks

1. Preheat the oven to 350ºF (180ºC).
2. Combine the olive oil with the honey. (Soften the honey in the microwave for 15 seconds, if necessary, for easier blending.) 3. In a shallow dish, combine the breadcrumbs, almonds, thyme, sea salt, and freshly ground pepper.
4. Coat the salmon steaks with the olive oil mixture, then the almond mixture.
5. Place on a baking sheet brushed with olive oil and bake 8–12 minutes, or until the almonds are lightly browned and the salmon is firm.

Per Serving: *calories: 634 / fat: 34g / protein: 69g / carbs: 12g / fiber: 2g / sodium: 289mg*

Lemon and Herb Fish Packets

Prep time: 10 minutes   Cook time: 5 minutes   Serves 4

- 1 cup water
- 4 (4-ounce / 113-g) halibut or other white fish fillets
- ½ teaspoon salt
- ½ teaspoon ground black pepper
- 1 small lemon, thinly sliced
- ¼ cup chopped fresh dill
- ¼ cup chopped fresh chives
- 2 tablespoons chopped fresh tarragon
- 2 tablespoons extra-virgin olive oil

1. Add water to the Instant Pot® and place the rack inside.
2. Season fish fillets with salt and pepper. Measure out four pieces of foil large enough to wrap around fish fillets. Lay fish fillets on foil. Top with lemon, dill, chives, and tarragon, and drizzle each with olive oil. Carefully wrap fish loosely in foil.
3. Place packets on rack. Close lid, set steam release to Sealing, press the Steam button, and set time to 5 minutes.
4. When the timer beeps, quick-release the pressure until the float valve drops. Press the Cancel button and open lid. Serve immediately.

Per Serving:calories: 185 / fat: 9g / protein: 23g / carbs: 0g / fiber: 0g / sodium: 355mg

Sicilian Kale and Tuna Bowl

Prep time: 5 minutes   Cook time: 15 minutes   Serves: 6

- 1 pound (454 g) kale, chopped, center ribs removed (about 12 cups)
- 3 tablespoons extra-virgin olive oil
- 1 cup chopped onion (about ½ medium onion)
- 3 garlic cloves, minced (about 1½ teaspoons)
- 1 (2¼-ounce / 35-g) can sliced olives, drained (about ½ cup)
- ¼ cup capers
- ¼ teaspoon crushed red pepper
- 2 teaspoons sugar
- 2 (6-ounce / 170-g) cans tuna in olive oil, undrained
- 1 (15-ounce / 425-g) can cannellini beans or great northern beans, drained and rinsed
- ¼ teaspoon freshly ground black pepper
- ¼ teaspoon kosher or sea salt

1. Fill a large stockpot three-quarters full of water, and bring to a boil. Add the kale and cook for 2 minutes. (This is to make the kale less bitter.) Drain the kale in a colander and set aside.
2. Set the empty pot back on the stove over medium heat, and pour in the oil. Add the onion and cook for 4 minutes, stirring often. Add the garlic and cook for 1 minute, stirring often. Add the olives, capers, and crushed red pepper, and cook for 1 minute, stirring often. Add the partially cooked kale and sugar, stirring until the kale is completely coated with oil. Cover the pot and cook for 8 minutes.
3. Remove the kale from the heat, mix in the tuna, beans, pepper, and salt, and serve.

Per Serving:calories: 323 / fat: 14g / protein: 26g / carbs: 26g / fiber: 7g / sodium: 653mg

Honeyed Salmon

Prep time: 10 minutes   Cook time: 1 hour   Serves 6

- 6 (6-ounce / 170-g) salmon fillets
- 2 tablespoons lime juice
- 1 tablespoon water
- 1 teaspoon ground ginger
- ½ cup honey
- 3 tablespoons worcestershire sauce
- 2 cloves garlic, minced
- ½ teaspoon black pepper

1. Place the salmon fillets in the slow cooker.
2. In medium bowl, whisk the honey, lime juice, Worcestershire sauce, water, garlic, ginger, and pepper. Pour sauce over salmon.
3. Cover and cook on high for 1 hour.

Per Serving:calories: 313 / fat: 8g / protein: 35g / carbs: 26g / fiber: 0g / sodium: 212mg

Moroccan Crusted Sea Bass

Prep time: 15 minutes   Cook time: 40 minutes   Serves 4

- 1½ teaspoons ground turmeric, divided
- ¾ teaspoon saffron
- ½ teaspoon ground cumin
- ¼ teaspoon kosher salt
- ¼ teaspoon freshly ground black pepper
- 1½ pounds (680 g) sea bass fillets, about ½ inch thick
- 8 tablespoons extra-virgin olive oil, divided
- 8 garlic cloves, divided (4 minced cloves and 4 sliced)
- 6 medium baby portobello mushrooms, chopped
- 1 large carrot, sliced on an angle
- 2 sun-dried tomatoes, thinly sliced (optional)
- 2 tablespoons tomato paste
- 1 (15-ounce / 425-g) can chickpeas, drained and rinsed
- 1½ cups low-sodium vegetable broth
- ¼ cup white wine
- 1 tablespoon ground coriander (optional)
- 1 cup sliced artichoke hearts marinated in olive oil
- ½ cup pitted kalamata olives
- ½ lemon, juiced
- ½ lemon, cut into thin rounds
- 4 to 5 rosemary sprigs or 2 tablespoons dried rosemary
- Fresh cilantro, for garnish

1. In a small mixing bowl, combine 1 teaspoon turmeric and the saffron and cumin. Season with salt and pepper. Season both sides of the fish with the spice mixture. Add 3 tablespoons of olive oil and work the fish to make sure it's well coated with the spices and the olive oil.
2. In a large sauté pan or skillet, heat 2 tablespoons of olive oil over medium heat until shimmering but not smoking. Sear the top side of the sea bass for about 1 minute, or until golden. Remove and set aside.
3. In the same skillet, add the minced garlic and cook very briefly, tossing regularly, until fragrant. Add the mushrooms, carrot, sun-dried tomatoes (if using), and tomato paste. Cook for 3 to 4 minutes over medium heat, tossing frequently, until fragrant. Add the chickpeas, broth, wine, coriander (if using), and the sliced garlic. Stir in the remaining ½ teaspoon ground turmeric. Raise the heat, if needed, and bring to a boil, then lower heat to simmer. Cover part of the way and let the sauce simmer for about 20 minutes, until thickened.
4. Carefully add the seared fish to the skillet. Ladle a bit of the sauce on top of the fish. Add the artichokes, olives, lemon juice and slices, and rosemary sprigs. Cook another 10 minutes or until the fish is fully cooked and flaky. Garnish with fresh cilantro.

Per Serving:calories: 696 / fat: 41g / protein: 48g / carbs: 37g / fiber: 9g / sodium: 810mg

Tuna Nuggets in Hoisin Sauce

Prep time: 15 minutes   Cook time: 5 to 7 minutes   Serves 4

- ½ cup hoisin sauce
- 2 teaspoons sesame oil
- 2 teaspoons dried lemongrass
- 2 tablespoons rice wine vinegar
- 1 teaspoon garlic powder
- ¼ teaspoon red pepper flakes
- ½ small onion, quartered and thinly sliced
- 8 ounces (227 g) fresh tuna, cut into 1-inch cubes
- Cooking spray
- 3 cups cooked jasmine rice

1. Mix the hoisin sauce, vinegar, sesame oil, and seasonings together.
2. Stir in the onions and tuna nuggets.
3. Spray a baking pan with nonstick spray and pour in tuna mixture.
4. Roast at 390ºF (199ºC) for 3 minutes. Stir gently.
5. Cook 2 minutes and stir again, checking for doneness. Tuna should be barely cooked through, just beginning to flake and still very moist. If necessary, continue cooking and stirring in 1-minute intervals until done.
6. Serve warm over hot jasmine rice.

Per Serving: *calories: 342 / fat: 7g / protein: 18g / carbs: 49g / fiber: 4g / sodium: 548mg*

Mixed Seafood Soup

Prep time: 15 minutes   Cook time: 22 minutes   Serves 8

- 2 tablespoons light olive oil
- 1 medium yellow onion, peeled and diced
- 1 medium red bell pepper, seeded and diced
- 3 cloves garlic, peeled and minced
- 1 tablespoon chopped fresh oregano
- ½ teaspoon Italian seasoning
- ½ teaspoon ground black pepper
- 2 tablespoons tomato paste
- ½ cup white wine
- 2 cups seafood stock
- 1 bay leaf
- ½ pound (227 g) medium shrimp, peeled and deveined
- ½ pound (227 g) fresh scallops
- ½ pound (227 g) fresh calamari rings
- 1 tablespoon lemon juice

1. Press the Sauté button on the Instant Pot® and heat oil. Add onion and bell pepper and cook until just tender, about 5 minutes. Add garlic, oregano, Italian seasoning, and pepper. Cook until fragrant, about 30 seconds. Add tomato paste and cook for 1 minute, then slowly pour in wine and scrape bottom of pot well. Press the Cancel button.
2. Add stock and bay leaf. Stir well. Close lid and set steam release to Sealing, then press the Manual button and set time to 5 minutes.
3. When the timer beeps, quick-release the pressure until the float valve drops. Open lid and stir in shrimp, scallops, calamari rings, and lemon juice. Press the Cancel button, then press the Sauté button and allow soup to simmer until seafood is cooked through, about 10 minutes. Remove and discard bay leaf. Serve hot.

Per Serving: *calories: 172 / fat: 7g / protein: 15g / carbs: 9g / fiber: 1g / sodium: 481mg*

Shrimp over Black Bean Linguine

Prep time: 10 minutes   Cook time: 15 minutes   Serves 4

- 1 pound (454 g) black bean linguine or spaghetti
- 1 pound (454 g) fresh shrimp, peeled and deveined
- 4 tablespoons extra-virgin olive oil
- 1 onion, finely chopped
- 3 garlic cloves, minced
- ¼ cup basil, cut into strips

1. Bring a large pot of water to a boil and cook the pasta according to the package instructions.
2. In the last 5 minutes of cooking the pasta, add the shrimp to the hot water and allow them to cook for 3 to 5 minutes. Once they turn pink, take them out of the hot water, and, if you think you may have overcooked them, run them under cool water. Set aside.
3. Reserve 1 cup of the pasta cooking water and drain the noodles. In the same pan, heat the oil over medium-high heat and cook the onion and garlic for 7 to 10 minutes. Once the onion is translucent, add the pasta back in and toss well.

4. Plate the pasta, then top with shrimp and garnish with basil.
Per Serving: calories: 668 / fat: 19g / protein: 57g / carbs: 73g / fiber: 31g / sodium: 615mg

South Indian Fried Fish

Prep time: 20 minutes   Cook time: 8 minutes   Serves 4

- 2 tablespoons olive oil
- 2 tablespoons fresh lime or lemon juice
- 1 teaspoon minced fresh ginger
- 1 clove garlic, minced
- 1 teaspoon ground turmeric
- ½ teaspoon kosher salt
- ¼ to ½ teaspoon cayenne pepper
- 1 pound (454 g) tilapia fillets (2 to 3 fillets)
- Olive oil spray
- Lime or lemon wedges (optional)

1. In a large bowl, combine the oil, lime juice, ginger, garlic, turmeric, salt, and cayenne. Stir until well combined; set aside.
2. Cut each tilapia fillet into three or four equal-size pieces. Add the fish to the bowl and gently mix until all of the fish is coated in the marinade. Marinate for 10 to 15 minutes at room temperature. (Don't marinate any longer or the acid in the lime juice will "cook" the fish.) 3. Spray the air fryer basket with olive oil spray. Place the fish in the basket and spray the fish. Set the air fryer to 325°F (163°C) for 3 minutes to partially cook the fish. Set the air fryer to 400°F (204°C) for 5 minutes to finish cooking and crisp up the fish. (Thinner pieces of fish will cook faster so you may want to check at the 3-minute mark of the second cooking time and remove those that are cooked through, and then add them back toward the end of the second cooking time to crisp.) 4. Carefully remove the fish from the basket. Serve hot, with lemon wedges if desired.
Per Serving: calories: 175 / fat: 9g / protein: 23g / carbs: 2g / fiber: 0g / sodium: 350mg

Southern Italian Seafood Stew in Tomato Broth

Prep time: 15 minutes　　　　Cook time: 1 hour 20 minutes　　　　Serves 6

- ½ cup olive oil
- 1 fennel bulb, cored and finely chopped
- 2 stalks celery, finely chopped
- 1 medium onion, finely chopped
- 1 tablespoon dried oregano
- ½ teaspoon crushed red pepper flakes
- 1½ pounds (680 g) cleaned squid, bodies cut into ½-inch rings, tentacles halved
- 2 cups dry white wine
- 1 (28-ounce / 794-g) can tomato purée
- 1 bay leaf
- 1 teaspoon salt
- ½ teaspoon freshly ground black pepper
- 1 cup bottled clam juice
- 1 pound (454 g) whole head-on prawns
- 1½ pounds (680 g) mussels, scrubbed
- 1 lemon, cut into wedges, for serving

1. In a large Dutch oven, heat the olive oil over medium-high heat. Add the fennel, celery, onion, oregano, and red pepper flakes and reduce the heat to medium. Cook, stirring occasionally, for about 15 minutes, until the vegetables soften. Stir in the squid, reduce the heat to low, and simmer for 15 minutes.
2. Add the wine to the pot, raise the heat to medium-high, and bring to a boil. Cook, stirring occasionally, until the wine has evaporated. Reduce the heat again to low and add the tomato purée, bay leaf, salt, and pepper. Cook gently, stirring every once in a while, for about 40 minutes, until the mixture becomes very thick.
3. Stir in 2 cups of water and the clam juice, raise the heat again to medium-high, and bring to a boil.
4. Add the shrimp and mussels and cook, covered, for 5 minutes or so, until the shells of the mussels have opened and the prawns are pink and cooked through.
5. To serve, ladle the seafood and broth into bowls and garnish with the lemon wedges. Serve hot.

Per Serving: *calories: 490 / fat: 23g / protein: 48g / carbs: 22g / fiber: 5g / sodium: 899mg*

Rosemary Salmon

Prep time: 5 minutes　　　　Cook time: 5 minutes　　　　Serves 4

- 1 cup water
- 4 (4-ounce / 113-g) salmon fillets
- ½ teaspoon salt
- ½ teaspoon ground black pepper
- 1 sprig rosemary, leaves stripped off and minced
- 2 tablespoons chopped fresh thyme
- 2 tablespoons extra-virgin olive oil
- 4 lemon wedges

1. Add water to the Instant Pot® and place rack inside.
2. Season fish fillets with salt and pepper. Measure out four pieces of foil large enough to wrap around fish fillets. Lay fish fillets on foil. Top with rosemary and thyme, then drizzle each with olive oil. Carefully wrap loosely in foil.
3. Place foil packets on rack. Close lid, set steam release to Sealing, press the Steam button, and set time to 5 minutes.
4. When the timer beeps, quick-release the pressure until the float valve drops. Press the Cancel button and open lid. Carefully remove packets to plates. Serve immediately with lemon wedges.

Per Serving: *calories: 160 / fat: 8g / protein: 24g / carbs: 0g / fiber: 0g / sodium: 445mg*

6

Snacks and Appetizers

Turmeric-Spiced Crunchy Chickpeas

Prep time: 15 minutes   Cook time: 30 minutes   Serves 4

- 2 (15-ounce / 425-g) cans organic chickpeas, drained and rinsed
- 3 tablespoons extra-virgin olive oil
- 2 teaspoons Turkish or smoked paprika
- 2 teaspoons turmeric
- ½ teaspoon dried oregano
- ½ teaspoon salt
- ¼ teaspoon ground ginger
- ⅛ teaspoon ground white pepper (optional)

1. Preheat the oven to 400°F(205°C). Line a baking sheet with parchment paper and set aside.
2. Completely dry the chickpeas. Lay the chickpeas out on a baking sheet, roll them around with paper towels, and allow them to air-dry. I usually let them dry for at least 2½ hours, but can also be left to dry overnight.
3. In a medium bowl, combine the olive oil, paprika, turmeric, oregano, salt, ginger, and white pepper (if using).
4. Add the dry chickpeas to the bowl and toss to combine.
5. Put the chickpeas on the prepared baking sheet and cook for 30 minutes, or until the chickpeas turn golden brown. At 15 minutes, move the chickpeas around on the baking sheet to avoid burning. Check every 10 minutes in case the chickpeas begin to crisp up before the full cooking time has elapsed.
6. Remove from the oven and set them aside to cool.

Per Serving: ½ cup: calories: 308 / fat: 13g / protein: 11g / carbs: 40g / fiber: 11g / sodium: 292mg

Skinny Fries

Prep time: 10 minutes   Cook time: 15 minutes per batch   Serves 2

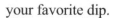

- 2 to 3 russet potatoes, peeled and cut into ¼-inch sticks
- 2 to 3 teaspoons olive or vegetable oil
- Salt, to taste

1. Cut the potatoes into ¼-inch strips. (A mandolin with a julienne blade is really helpful here.) Rinse the potatoes with cold water several times and let them soak in cold water for at least 10 minutes or as long as overnight.
2. Preheat the air fryer to 380°F (193°C).
3. Drain and dry the potato sticks really well, using a clean kitchen towel. Toss the fries with the oil in a bowl and then air fry the fries in two batches at 380°F (193°C) for 15 minutes, shaking the basket a couple of times while they cook.
4. Add the first batch of French fries back into the air fryer basket with the finishing batch and let everything warm through for a few minutes. As soon as the fries are done, season them with salt and transfer to a plate or basket. Serve them warm with ketchup or your favorite dip.

Per Serving: *calories: 207 / fat: 5g / protein: 5g / carbs: 38g / fiber: 3g / sodium: 11mg*

Cheese-Stuffed Dates

Prep time: 10 minutes   Cook time: 10 minutes   Serves 4

- 2 ounces (57 g) low-fat cream cheese, at room temperature
- 2 tablespoons sweet pickle relish
- 1 tablespoon low-fat plain Greek yogurt
- 1 teaspoon finely chopped fresh chives
- ¼ teaspoon kosher salt
- ⅛ teaspoon ground black pepper
- Dash of hot sauce
- 2 tablespoons pistachios, chopped
- 8 Medjool dates, pitted and halved

1. In a small bowl, stir together the cream cheese, relish, yogurt, chives, salt, pepper, and hot sauce.
2. Put the pistachios on a clean plate. Put the cream cheese mixture into a resealable plastic bag, and snip off 1 corner of the bag. Pipe the cream cheese mixture into the date halves and press the tops into the pistachios to coat.

*Per Serving:*calories: 196 / fat: 4g / protein: 3g / carbs: 41g / fiber: 4g / sodium: 294mg

Cheesy Dates

Prep time: 15 minutes   Cook time: 10 minutes   Serves 12 to 15

- 1 cup pecans, shells removed
- 1 (8-ounce / 227-g) container mascarpone cheese
- 20 Medjool dates

1. Preheat the oven to 350°F(180°C). Put the pecans on a baking sheet and bake for 5 to 6 minutes, until lightly toasted and aromatic. Take the pecans out of the oven and let cool for 5 minutes.
2. Once cooled, put the pecans in a food processor fitted with a chopping blade and chop until they resemble the texture of bulgur wheat or coarse sugar.
3. Reserve ¼ cup of ground pecans in a small bowl. Pour the remaining chopped pecans into a larger bowl and add the mascarpone cheese.
4. Using a spatula, mix the cheese with the pecans until evenly combined.
5. Spoon the cheese mixture into a piping bag.
6. Using a knife, cut one side of the date lengthwise, from the stem to the bottom. Gently open and remove the pit.
7. Using the piping bag, squeeze a generous amount of the cheese mixture into the date where the pit used to be. Close up the date and repeat with the remaining dates.
8. Dip any exposed cheese from the stuffed dates into the reserved chopped pecans to cover it up.
9. Set the dates on a serving plate; serve immediately or chill in the fridge until you are ready to serve.

*Per Serving:*calories: 253 / fat: 4g / protein: 2g / carbs: 31g / fiber: 4g / sodium: 7mg

Citrus-Marinated Olives

Prep time: 10 minutes   Cook time: 0 minutes   Makes 2 cups

- 2 cups mixed green olives with pits
- ¼ cup red wine vinegar
- ¼ cup extra-virgin olive oil
- 4 garlic cloves, finely minced
- Zest and juice of 2 clementines or 1 large orange
- 1 teaspoon red pepper flakes
- 2 bay leaves
- ½ teaspoon ground cumin
- ½ teaspoon ground allspice

1. In a large glass bowl or jar, combine the olives, vinegar, oil, garlic, orange zest and juice, red pepper flakes, bay leaves, cumin, and allspice and mix well. Cover and refrigerate for at least 4 hours or up to a week to allow the olives to marinate, tossing again before serving.

Per Serving: *¼ cup: calories: 112 / fat: 10g / protein: 1g / carbs: 5g / fiber: 2g / sodium: 248mg*

Vegetable Pot Stickers

Prep time: 12 minutes   Cook time: 11 to 18 minutes   Makes 12 pot stickers

- 1 cup shredded red cabbage
- ¼ cup chopped button mushrooms
- ¼ cup grated carrot
- 2 tablespoons minced onion
- 2 garlic cloves, minced
- 2 teaspoons grated fresh ginger
- 12 gyoza/pot sticker wrappers
- 2½ teaspoons olive oil, divided

1. In a baking pan, combine the red cabbage, mushrooms, carrot, onion, garlic, and ginger. Add 1 tablespoon of water. Place in the air fryer and air fry at 370ºF (188ºC) for 3 to 6 minutes, until the vegetables are crisp-tender. Drain and set aside.
2. Working one at a time, place the pot sticker wrappers on a work surface. Top each wrapper with a scant 1 tablespoon of the filling. Fold half of the wrapper over the other half to form a half circle. Dab one edge with water and press both edges together.
3. To another pan, add 1¼ teaspoons of olive oil. Put half of the pot stickers, seam-side up, in the pan. Air fry for 5 minutes, or until the bottoms are light golden brown. Add 1 tablespoon of water and return the pan to the air fryer.
4. Air fry for 4 to 6 minutes more, or until hot. Repeat with the remaining pot stickers, remaining 1¼ teaspoons of oil, and another tablespoon of water. Serve immediately.

Per Serving: *1 pot stickers: calories: 36 / fat: 1g / protein: 1g / carbs: 6g / fiber: 0g / sodium: 49mg*

Burrata Caprese Stack

Prep time: 5 minutes | Cook time: 0 minutes | Serves 4

- 1 large organic tomato, preferably heirloom
- ½ teaspoon salt
- ¼ teaspoon freshly ground black pepper
- 1 (4 ounces / 113 g) ball burrata cheese
- 8 fresh basil leaves, thinly sliced
- 2 tablespoons extra-virgin olive oil
- 1 tablespoon red wine or balsamic vinegar

1. Slice the tomato into 4 thick slices, removing any tough center core and sprinkle with salt and pepper. Place the tomatoes, seasoned-side up, on a plate.
2. On a separate rimmed plate, slice the burrata into 4 thick slices and place one slice on top of each tomato slice. Top each with one-quarter of the basil and pour any reserved burrata cream from the rimmed plate over top.
3. Drizzle with olive oil and vinegar and serve with a fork and knife.

Per Serving: calories: 109 / fat: 7g / protein: 9g / carbs: 3g / fiber: 1g / sodium: 504mg

Italian Crepe with Herbs and Onion

Prep time: 15 minutes | Cook time: 20 minutes per crepe | Serves 6

- 2 cups cold water
- 1 cup chickpea flour
- ½ teaspoon kosher salt
- ¼ teaspoon freshly ground black pepper
- 3½ tablespoons extra-virgin olive oil, divided
- ½ onion, julienned
- ½ cup fresh herbs, chopped (thyme, sage, and rosemary are all nice on their own or as a mix)

1. In a large bowl, whisk together the water, flour, salt, and black pepper. Add 2 tablespoons of the olive oil and whisk. Let the batter sit at room temperature for at least 30 minutes.
2. Preheat the oven to 450ºF (235ºC). Place a 12-inch cast-iron pan or oven-safe skillet in the oven to warm as the oven comes to temperature.
3. Remove the hot pan from the oven carefully, add ½ tablespoon of the olive oil and one-third of the onion, stir, and place the pan back in the oven. Cook, stirring occasionally, until the onions are golden brown, 5 to 8 minutes.
4. Remove the pan from the oven and pour in one-third of the batter (about 1 cup), sprinkle with one-third of the herbs, and put it back in the oven. Bake for 10 minutes, or until firm and the edges are set.
5. Increase the oven setting to broil and cook 3 to 5 minutes, or until golden brown. Slide the crepe onto the cutting board and repeat twice more. Halve the crepes and cut into wedges. Serve warm or at room temperature.

Per Serving: calories: 135 / fat: 9g / protein: 4g / carbs: 11g / fiber: 2g / sodium: 105mg

Taco-Spiced Chickpeas

Prep time: 5 minutes   Cook time: 17 minutes   Serves 3

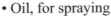

- Oil, for spraying
- 1 (15½-ounce / 439-g) can chickpeas, drained
- 1 teaspoon chili powder
- ½ teaspoon ground cumin
- ½ teaspoon salt
- ½ teaspoon granulated garlic
- 2 teaspoons lime juice

1. Line the air fryer basket with parchment and spray lightly with oil. Place the chickpeas in the prepared basket.
2. Air fry at 390ºF (199ºC) for 17 minutes, shaking or stirring the chickpeas and spraying lightly with oil every 5 to 7 minutes.
3. In a small bowl, mix together the chili powder, cumin, salt, and garlic.
4. When 2 to 3 minutes of cooking time remain, sprinkle half of the seasoning mix over the chickpeas. Finish cooking.
5. Transfer the chickpeas to a medium bowl and toss with the remaining seasoning mix and the lime juice. Serve immediately.

Per Serving:calories: 208 / fat: 4g / protein: 11g / carbs: 34g / fiber: 10g / sodium: 725mg

Stuffed Fried Mushrooms

Prep time: 20 minutes   Cook time: 10 to 11 minutes   Serves 10

- ½ cup panko bread crumbs
- ½ teaspoon freshly ground black pepper
- ½ teaspoon onion powder
- ½ teaspoon cayenne pepper
- 1 (8-ounce / 227-g) package cream cheese, at room temperature
- 20 cremini or button mushrooms, stemmed
- 1 to 2 tablespoons oil

1. In a medium bowl, whisk the bread crumbs, black pepper, onion powder, and cayenne until blended.
2. Add the cream cheese and mix until well blended. Fill each mushroom top with 1 teaspoon of the cream cheese mixture 3. Preheat the air fryer to 360ºF (182ºC). Line the air fryer basket with a piece of parchment paper.
4. Place the mushrooms on the parchment and spritz with oil.
5. Cook for 5 minutes. Shake the basket and cook for 5 to 6 minutes more until the filling is firm and the mushrooms are soft.

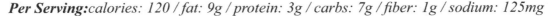

Per Serving:calories: 120 / fat: 9g / protein: 3g / carbs: 7g / fiber: 1g / sodium: 125mg

7

Vegetables and Sides

Fried Zucchini Salad

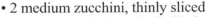

Prep time: 10 minutes   Cook time: 5 to 7 minutes   Serves 4

- 2 medium zucchini, thinly sliced
- 5 tablespoons olive oil, divided
- ¼ cup chopped fresh parsley
- 2 tablespoons chopped fresh mint
- Zest and juice of ½ lemon
- 1 clove garlic, minced
- ¼ cup crumbled feta cheese
- Freshly ground black pepper, to taste

1. Preheat the air fryer to 400°F (204°C).
2. In a large bowl, toss the zucchini slices with 1 tablespoon of the olive oil.
3. Working in batches if necessary, arrange the zucchini slices in an even layer in the air fryer basket. Pausing halfway through the cooking time to shake the basket, air fry for 5 to 7 minutes until soft and lightly browned on each side.
4. Meanwhile, in a small bowl, combine the remaining 4 tablespoons olive oil, parsley, mint, lemon zest, lemon juice, and garlic.
5. Arrange the zucchini on a plate and drizzle with the dressing. Sprinkle the feta and black pepper on top. Serve warm or at room temperature.

Per Serving: *calories: 194 / fat: 19g / protein: 3g / carbs: 4g / fiber: 1g / sodium: 96mg*

Stuffed Artichokes

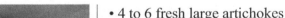

Prep time: 20 minutes   Cook time: 5 to 7 hours   Serves 4 to 6

- 4 to 6 fresh large artichokes
- ½ cup bread crumbs
- ½ cup grated Parmesan cheese or Romano cheese
- 4 garlic cloves, minced
- ½ teaspoon sea salt
- ½ teaspoon freshly ground black pepper
- ¼ cup water
- 2 tablespoons extra-virgin olive oil
- 2 tablespoons chopped fresh parsley for garnish (optional)

1. To trim and prepare the artichokes, cut off the bottom along with 1 inch from the top of each artichoke. Pull off and discard the lowest leaves nearest the stem end. Trim off any pointy tips of artichoke leaves that are poking out. Set aside.
2. In a small bowl, stir together the bread crumbs, Parmesan cheese, garlic, salt, and pepper.
3. Spread apart the artichoke leaves and stuff the bread-crumb mixture into the spaces, down to the base.
4. Pour the water into a slow cooker.
5. Place the artichokes in the slow cooker in a single layer. Drizzle the olive oil over the artichokes.
6. Cover the cooker and cook for 5 to 7 hours on Low heat, or until the artichokes are tender.
7. Garnish with fresh parsley if desired.

Per Serving: *calories: 224 / fat: 12g / protein: 12g / carbs: 23g / fiber: 8g / sodium: 883mg*

Roasted Brussels Sprouts with Delicata Squash and Balsamic Glaze

Prep time: 10 minutes   Cook time: 30 minutes   Serves 2

- ½ pound (227 g) Brussels sprouts, ends trimmed and outer leaves removed
- 1 medium delicata squash, halved lengthwise, seeded, and cut into 1-inch pieces
- 1 cup fresh cranberries
- 2 teaspoons olive oil
- Salt
- Freshly ground black pepper
- ½ cup balsamic vinegar
- 2 tablespoons roasted pumpkin seeds
- 2 tablespoons fresh pomegranate arils (seeds)

1. Preheat oven to 400°F (205°C) and set the rack to the middle position. Line a sheet pan with parchment paper.
2. Combine the Brussels sprouts, squash, and cranberries in a large bowl. Drizzle with olive oil, and season liberally with salt and pepper. Toss well to coat and arrange in a single layer on the sheet pan.
3. Roast for 30 minutes, turning vegetables halfway through, or until Brussels sprouts turn brown and crisp in spots and squash has golden-brown spots.
4. While vegetables are roasting, prepare the balsamic glaze by simmering the vinegar for 10 to 12 minutes, or until mixture has reduced to about ¼ cup and turns a syrupy consistency.
5. Remove the vegetables from the oven, drizzle with balsamic syrup, and sprinkle with pumpkin seeds and pomegranate arils before serving.

Per Serving: *calories: 201 / fat: 7g / protein: 6g / carbs: 21g / fiber: 8g / sodium: 34mg*

Spinach and Sweet Pepper Poppers

Prep time: 10 minutes   Cook time: 8 minutes   Makes 16 poppers

- 4 ounces (113 g) cream cheese, softened
- 1 cup chopped fresh spinach leaves
- ½ teaspoon garlic powder
- 8 mini sweet bell peppers, tops removed, seeded, and halved lengthwise

1. In a medium bowl, mix cream cheese, spinach, and garlic powder. Place 1 tablespoon mixture into each sweet pepper half and press down to smooth.
2. Place poppers into ungreased air fryer basket. Adjust the temperature to 400°F (204°C) and air fry for 8 minutes. Poppers will be done when cheese is browned on top and peppers are tender-crisp. Serve warm.

Per Serving: *calories: 31 / fat: 2g / protein: 1g / carbs: 3g / fiber: 0g / sodium: 34mg*

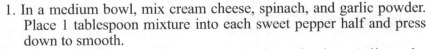

Potato Vegetable Hash

Prep time: 20 minutes   Cook time: 5 to 7 hours   Serves 4

- 1½ pounds (680 g) red potatoes, diced
- 8 ounces (227 g) green beans, trimmed and cut into ½-inch pieces
- 4 ounces (113 g) mushrooms, chopped
- 1 large tomato, chopped
- 1 large zucchini, diced
- 1 small onion, diced
- 1 red bell pepper, seeded and chopped
- ⅓ cup low-sodium vegetable broth
- 1 teaspoon sea salt
- ½ teaspoon garlic powder
- ½ teaspoon freshly ground black pepper
- ¼ teaspoon red pepper flakes
- ¼ cup shredded cheese of your choice (optional)

1. In a slow cooker, combine the potatoes, green beans, mushrooms, tomato, zucchini, onion, bell pepper, vegetable broth, salt, garlic powder, black pepper, and red pepper flakes. Stir to mix well.
2. Cover the cooker and cook for 5 to 7 hours on Low heat.
3. Garnish with cheese for serving (if using).

Per Serving:*calories: 183 / fat: 1g / protein: 7g / carbs: 41g / fiber: 8g / sodium: 642mg*

Honey and Spice Glazed Carrots

Prep time: 5 minutes   Cook time: 5 minutes   Serves 4

- 4 large carrots, peeled and sliced on the diagonal into ½-inch-thick rounds
- 1 teaspoon ground cinnamon
- 1 teaspoon ground ginger
- 3 tablespoons olive oil
- ½ cup honey
- 1 tablespoon red wine vinegar
- 1 tablespoon chopped flat-leaf parsley
- 1 tablespoon chopped cilantro
- 2 tablespoons toasted pine nuts

1. Bring a large saucepan of lightly salted water to a boil and add the carrots. Cover and cook for about 5 minutes, until the carrots are just tender. Drain in a colander, then transfer to a medium bowl.
2. Add the cinnamon, ginger, olive oil, honey, and vinegar and toss to combine well. Add the parsley and cilantro and toss again to incorporate. Garnish with the pine nuts. Serve immediately or let cool to room temperature.

Per Serving:*calories: 281 / fat: 14g / protein: 1g / carbs: 43g / fiber: 2g / sodium: 48mg*

Greek Bean Soup

Prep time: 10 minutes | Cook time: 45 minutes | Serves 4

- 2 tablespoons olive oil
- 1 large onion, chopped
- 1 (15-ounce / 425-g) can diced tomatoes
- 1 (15-ounce / 425-g) can great northern beans, drained and rinsed
- 2 celery stalks, chopped
- 2 carrots, cut into long ribbons
- ⅓ teaspoon chopped fresh thyme
- ¼ cup chopped fresh Italian parsley
- 1 bay leaf
- Sea salt
- Freshly ground black pepper

1. In a Dutch oven, heat the olive oil over medium-high heat. Add the onion and sauté for 4 minutes, or until softened. Add the tomatoes, beans, celery, carrots, thyme, parsley, and bay leaf, then add water to cover by about 2 inches.
2. Bring the soup to a boil, reduce the heat to low, cover, and simmer for 30 minutes, or until the vegetables are tender.
3. Remove the bay leaf, season with salt and pepper, and serve.

Per Serving: *calories: 185 / fat: 7g / protein: 7g / carbs: 25g / fiber: 8g / sodium: 155mg*

Greek Garlic Dip

Prep time: 10 minutes | Cook time: 30 minutes | Serves 4

- 2 potatoes (about 1 pound / 454 g), peeled and quartered
- ½ cup olive oil
- ¼ cup freshly squeezed lemon juice
- 4 garlic cloves, minced
- Sea salt
- Freshly ground black pepper

1. Place the potatoes in a large saucepan and fill the pan three-quarters full with water. Bring the water to a boil over medium-high heat, then reduce the heat to medium and cook the potatoes until fork-tender, 20 to 30 minutes.
2. While the potatoes are boiling, in a medium bowl, stir together the olive oil, lemon juice, and garlic; set aside.
3. Drain the potatoes and return them to the saucepan. Pour in the oil mixture and mash with a potato masher or a fork until well combined and smooth. Taste and season with salt and pepper. Serve.

Per Serving: *calories: 334 / fat: 27g / protein: 3g / carbs: 22g / fiber: 3g / sodium: 47mg*

Lemon-Thyme Asparagus

Prep time: 5 minutes   Cook time: 4 to 8 minutes   Serves 4

- 1 pound (454 g) asparagus, woody ends trimmed off
- 1 tablespoon avocado oil
- ½ teaspoon dried thyme or ½ tablespoon chopped fresh thyme
- Sea salt and freshly ground black pepper, to taste
- 2 ounces (57 g) goat cheese, crumbled
- Zest and juice of 1 lemon
- Flaky sea salt, for serving (optional)

1. In a medium bowl, toss together the asparagus, avocado oil, and thyme, and season with sea salt and pepper.
2. Place the asparagus in the air fryer basket in a single layer. Set the air fryer to 400°F (204°C) and air fry for 4 to 8 minutes, to your desired doneness.
3. Transfer to a serving platter. Top with the goat cheese, lemon zest, and lemon juice. If desired, season with a pinch of flaky salt.

Per Serving: calories: 121 / fat: 9g / protein: 7g / carbs: 6g / fiber: 3g / sodium: 208mg

Baked Turkey Kibbeh

Prep time: 15 minutes   Cook time: 45 minutes   Serves 8

- Outer Layer:
- 1½ cups bulgur wheat
- 1 yellow onion, grated on a box grater
- ½ cup finely chopped fresh mint
- ½ teaspoon ground cinnamon
- ¼ teaspoon ground black pepper
- 4 tablespoons olive oil, divided
- 3 cloves garlic, minced
- ¼ cup finely chopped fresh flat-leaf parsley
- ½ cup pine nuts, toasted
- ½ teaspoon kosher salt
- Assembly and Serving:
- 1 tablespoon olive oil
- 1¼ pounds (567 g) ground turkey
- 1 teaspoon ground allspice
- 1 teaspoon kosher salt
- Filling:
- 1 yellow onion, finely chopped
- 1 pound (454 g) ground turkey
- ½ teaspoon ground allspice
- ¼ teaspoon ground black pepper
- ¼ cup thinly sliced fresh mint
- 8 tablespoons low-fat Greek yogurt or labneh

1. To make the outer layer: Soak the bulgur overnight in a bowl with enough water to cover by 2'.
2. Drain, squeezing the bulgur until there is no excess moisture. Transfer to a large bowl.
3. With your hands, mix in the turkey, onion, mint, allspice, cinnamon, salt, and pepper until thoroughly combined.
4. To make the filling: In a medium cast-iron skillet over medium heat, warm 2 tablespoons of the oil. Cook the onion and garlic until translucent, about 8 minutes. Add the turkey and cook until no longer pink, about 5 minutes.
5. Stir in the parsley, pine nuts, allspice, salt, and pepper. Drizzle in the remaining 2 tablespoons oil. Transfer to a bowl and wipe out the skillet.
6. To assemble the kibbeh: Preheat an oven to 350°F(180°C). Lightly coat the cast-iron skillet with olive oil.
7. Press half of the outer layer into the bottom of the skillet in an even layer about ¾' thick. Spread the filling evenly over the top. Using wet fingers, use the remaining half of the outer layer to cover the filling. Once the filling is completely covered, smooth with wet hands.
8. Score the surface of the kibbeh into 8 wedges to make it easier to cut and portion after baking. Drizzle the oil over the top and bake until deep brown, about 30 minutes.
9. Serve hot with the yogurt or labneh and a sprinkle of the mint.

Per Serving: calories: 395 / fat: 21g / protein: 31g / carbs: 24g / fiber: 6g / sodium: 462mg

Rice Pilaf with Dill

Prep time: 15 minutes   Cook time: 25 minutes   Serves 6

- 2 tablespoons olive oil
- 1 carrot, finely chopped (about ¾ cup)
- 2 leeks, halved lengthwise, washed, well drained, and sliced in half-moons
- ½ teaspoon salt
- ¼ teaspoon freshly ground black pepper
- 2 tablespoons chopped fresh dill
- 1 cup low-sodium vegetable broth or water
- ½ cup basmati rice

1. In a 2-or 3-quart saucepan, heat the olive oil over medium heat. Add the carrot, leeks, salt, pepper, and 1 tablespoon of the dill. Cover and cook for 6 to 8 minutes, stirring once, to soften all the vegetables but not brown them.
2. Add the broth or water and bring to a boil. Stir in the rice, reduce the heat to maintain a simmer, cover, and cook for 15 minutes. Remove from the heat; let stand, covered, for 10 minutes.
3. Fluff the rice with fork. Stir in the remaining 1 tablespoon dill and serve.

Per Serving:*1 cup: calories: 100 / fat: 7g / protein: 2g / carbs: 11g / fiber: 4g / sodium: 209mg*

Lemony Orzo

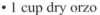

Prep time: 5 minutes   Cook time: 5 minutes   Yield 2 cups

- 1 cup dry orzo
- 1 cup halved grape tomatoes
- 1 (6-ounce / 170-g) bag baby spinach
- 2 tablespoons extra-virgin olive oil
- ¼ teaspoon salt
- Freshly ground black pepper
- ¾ cup crumbled feta cheese
- 1 lemon, juiced and zested

1. Bring a medium pot of water to a boil. Stir in the orzo and cook uncovered for 8 minutes. Drain the water, then return the orzo to medium heat.
2. Add in the tomatoes and spinach and cook until the spinach is wilted. Add the oil, salt, and pepper and mix well. Top the dish with feta, lemon juice, and lemon zest, then toss one or two more times and enjoy!

Per Serving: *½ cup: calories: 273 / fat: 13g / protein: 10g / carbs: 32g / fiber: 6g / sodium: 445mg*

8

Vegetarian Mains

Three-Cheese Zucchini Boats

Prep time: 15 minutes   Cook time: 20 minutes   Serves 2

- 2 medium zucchini
- 1 tablespoon avocado oil
- ¼ cup low-carb, no-sugar-added pasta sauce
- ¼ cup full-fat ricotta cheese
- ¼ cup shredded Mozzarella cheese
- ¼ teaspoon dried oregano
- ¼ teaspoon garlic powder
- ½ teaspoon dried parsley
- 2 tablespoons grated vegetarian Parmesan cheese

1. Cut off 1 inch from the top and bottom of each zucchini. Slice zucchini in half lengthwise and use a spoon to scoop out a bit of the inside, making room for filling. Brush with oil and spoon 2 tablespoons pasta sauce into each shell.
2. In a medium bowl, mix ricotta, Mozzarella, oregano, garlic powder, and parsley. Spoon the mixture into each zucchini shell. Place stuffed zucchini shells into the air fryer basket.
3. Adjust the temperature to 350°F (177°C) and air fry for 20 minutes.
4. To remove from the basket, use tongs or a spatula and carefully lift out. Top with Parmesan. Serve immediately.

Per Serving:calories: 208 / fat: 14g / protein: 12g / carbs: 11g / fiber: 3g / sodium: 247mg

Freekeh, Chickpea, and Herb Salad

Prep time: 15 minutes   Cook time: 10 minutes   Serves 4
                                                                to 6

- 1 (15-ounce / 425-g) can chickpeas, rinsed and drained
- 1 cup cooked freekeh
- 1 cup thinly sliced celery
- 1 bunch scallions, both white and green parts, finely chopped
- ½ cup chopped fresh flat-leaf parsley
- ¼ cup chopped fresh mint
- 3 tablespoons chopped celery leaves
- ½ teaspoon kosher salt
- ⅓ cup extra-virgin olive oil
- ¼ cup freshly squeezed lemon juice
- ¼ teaspoon cumin seeds
- 1 teaspoon garlic powder

1. In a large bowl, combine the chickpeas, freekeh, celery, scallions, parsley, mint, celery leaves, and salt and toss lightly.
2. In a small bowl, whisk together the olive oil, lemon juice, cumin seeds, and garlic powder. Once combined, add to freekeh salad.

Per Serving:calories: 350 / fat: 19g / protein: 9g / carbs: 38g / fiber: 9g / sodium: 329mg

Roasted Veggie Bowl

Prep time: 10 minutes   Cook time: 15 minutes   Serves 2

- 1 cup broccoli florets
- 1 cup quartered Brussels sprouts
- ½ cup cauliflower florets
- ¼ medium white onion, peeled and sliced ¼ inch thick
- ½ medium green bell pepper, seeded and sliced ¼ inch thick
- 1 tablespoon coconut oil
- 2 teaspoons chili powder
- ½ teaspoon garlic powder
- ½ teaspoon cumin

1. Toss all ingredients together in a large bowl until vegetables are fully coated with oil and seasoning.
2. Pour vegetables into the air fryer basket.
3. Adjust the temperature to 360ºF (182ºC) and roast for 15 minutes.
4. Shake two or three times during cooking. Serve warm.

Per Serving:*calories: 112 / fat: 8g / protein: 4g / carbs: 11g / fiber: 5g / sodium: 106mg*

Crustless Spanakopita

Prep time: 15 minutes   Cook time: 45 minutes   Serves 6

- 12 tablespoons extra-virgin olive oil, divided
- 1 small yellow onion, diced
- 1 (32-ounce / 907-g) bag frozen chopped spinach, thawed, fully drained, and patted dry (about 4 cups)
- 4 garlic cloves, minced
- ½ teaspoon salt
- ½ teaspoon freshly ground black pepper
- 1 cup whole-milk ricotta cheese
- 4 large eggs
- ¾ cup crumbled traditional feta cheese
- ¼ cup pine nuts

1. Preheat the oven to 375ºF (190ºC).
2. In a large skillet, heat 4 tablespoons olive oil over medium-high heat. Add the onion and sauté until softened, 6 to 8 minutes.
3. Add the spinach, garlic, salt, and pepper and sauté another 5 minutes. Remove from the heat and allow to cool slightly.
4. In a medium bowl, whisk together the ricotta and eggs. Add to the cooled spinach and stir to combine.
5. Pour 4 tablespoons olive oil in the bottom of a 9-by-13-inch glass baking dish and swirl to coat the bottom and sides. Add the spinach-ricotta mixture and spread into an even layer.
6. Bake for 20 minutes or until the mixture begins to set. Remove from the oven and crumble the feta evenly across the top of the spinach. Add the pine nuts and drizzle with the remaining 4 tablespoons olive oil. Return to the oven and bake for an additional 15 to 20 minutes, or until the spinach is fully set and the top is starting to turn golden brown. Allow to cool slightly before cutting to serve.

Per Serving:*calories: 497 / fat: 44g / protein: 18g / carbs: 11g / fiber: 5g / sodium: 561mg*

Caprese Eggplant Stacks

Prep time: 5 minutes   Cook time: 12 minutes   Serves 4

- 1 medium eggplant, cut into ¼-inch slices
- 2 large tomatoes, cut into ¼-inch slices
- 4 ounces (113 g) fresh Mozzarella, cut into ½-ounce / 14-g slices
- 2 tablespoons olive oil
- ¼ cup fresh basil, sliced

1. In a baking dish, place four slices of eggplant on the bottom. Place a slice of tomato on top of each eggplant round, then Mozzarella, then eggplant. Repeat as necessary.
2. Drizzle with olive oil. Cover dish with foil and place dish into the air fryer basket.
3. Adjust the temperature to 350ºF (177ºC) and bake for 12 minutes.
4. When done, eggplant will be tender. Garnish with fresh basil to serve.

Per Serving:calories: 97 / fat: 7g / protein: 2g / carbs: 8g / fiber: 4g / sodium: 11mg

Tortellini in Red Pepper Sauce

Prep time: 15 minutes   Cook time: 10 minutes   Serves 4

- 1 (16-ounce / 454-g) container fresh cheese tortellini (usually green and white pasta)
- 1 (16-ounce / 454-g) jar roasted red peppers, drained
- 1 teaspoon garlic powder
- ¼ cup tahini
- 1 tablespoon red pepper oil (optional)

1. Bring a large pot of water to a boil and cook the tortellini according to package directions.
2. In a blender, combine the red peppers with the garlic powder and process until smooth. Once blended, add the tahini until the sauce is thickened. If the sauce gets too thick, add up to 1 tablespoon red pepper oil (if using).
3. Once tortellini are cooked, drain and leave pasta in colander. Add the sauce to the bottom of the empty pot and heat for 2 minutes. Then, add the tortellini back into the pot and cook for 2 more minutes. Serve and enjoy!

Per Serving:calories: 350 / fat: 11g / protein: 12g / carbs: 46g / fiber: 4g / sodium: 192mg

Crustless Spinach Cheese Pie

Prep time: 10 minutes Cook time: 20 minutes Serves 4

- 6 large eggs
- ¼ cup heavy whipping cream
- 1 cup frozen chopped spinach, drained
- 1 cup shredded sharp Cheddar cheese
- ¼ cup diced yellow onion

1. In a medium bowl, whisk eggs and add cream. Add remaining ingredients to bowl.
2. Pour into a round baking dish. Place into the air fryer basket.
3. Adjust the temperature to 320ºF (160ºC) and bake for 20 minutes.
4. Eggs will be firm and slightly browned when cooked. Serve immediately.

Per Serving:calories: 263 / fat: 20g / protein: 18g / carbs: 4g / fiber: 1g / sodium: 321mg

Fava Bean Purée with Chicory

Prep time: 5 minutes Cook time: 2 hours 10 minutes Serves 4

- ½ pound (227 g) dried fava beans, soaked in water overnight and drained
- 1 pound (454 g) chicory leaves
- ¼ cup olive oil
- 1 small onion, chopped
- 1 clove garlic, minced
- Salt

1. In a saucepan, cover the fava beans by at least an inch of water and bring to a boil over medium-high heat. Reduce the heat to low, cover, and simmer until very tender, about 2 hours. Check the pot from time to time to make sure there is enough water and add more as needed.
2. Drain off any excess water and then mash the beans with a potato masher.
3. While the beans are cooking, bring a large pot of salted water to a boil. Add the chicory and cook for about 3 minutes, until tender. Drain.
4. In a medium skillet, heat the olive oil over medium-high heat. Add the onion and a pinch of salt and cook, stirring frequently, until softened and beginning to brown, about 5 minutes. Add the garlic and cook, stirring, for another minute. Transfer half of the onion mixture, along with the oil, to the bowl with the mashed beans and stir to mix. Taste and add salt as needed.
5. Serve the purée topped with some of the remaining onions and oil, with the chicory leaves on the side.

Per Serving:calories: 336 / fat: 14g / protein: 17g / carbs: 40g / fiber: 19g / sodium: 59mg

9
Desserts

Slow-Cooked Fruit Medley

Prep time: 10 minutes   Cook time: 3 to 5 hours   Serves 4 to 6

- Nonstick cooking spray
- 1 pound (454 g) fresh or frozen fruit of your choice, stemmed and chopped as needed
- ⅓ cup almond milk or low-sugar fruit juice of your choice
- ½ cup honey

1. Generously coat a slow cooker with cooking spray, or line the bottom and sides with parchment paper or aluminum foil.
2. In a slow cooker, combine the fruit and milk. Gently stir to mix.
3. Drizzle the fruit with the honey.
4. Cover the cooker and cook for 3 to 5 hours on Low heat.

Per Serving: calories: 192 / fat: 0g / protein: 1g / carbs: 50g / fiber: 3g / sodium: 27mg

Avocado-Orange Fruit Salad

Prep time: 10 minutes   Cook time: 0 minutes   Serves 5 to 6

- 2 large Gala apples, chopped
- 2 oranges, segmented and chopped
- ⅓ cup sliced almonds
- ½ cup honey
- 1 tablespoon extra-virgin olive oil
- ½ teaspoon grated orange zest
- 1 large avocado, semi-ripened, medium diced

1. In a large bowl, combine the apples, oranges, and almonds. Mix gently.
2. In a small bowl, whisk the honey, oil, and orange zest. Set aside.
3. Drizzle the orange zest mix over the fruit salad and toss. Add the avocado and toss gently one more time.

Per Serving: calories: 296 / fat: 12g / protein: 3g / carbs: 51g / fiber: 7g / sodium: 4mg

Fresh Figs with Chocolate Sauce

Prep time: 5 minutes   Cook time: 0 minutes   Serves 4

- ¼ cup honey
- 2 tablespoons cocoa powder
- 8 fresh figs

1. Combine the honey and cocoa powder in a small bowl, and mix well to form a syrup.
2. Cut the figs in half and place cut side up. Drizzle with the syrup and serve.

Per Serving:*calories: 112 / fat: 1g / protein: 1g / carbs: 30g / fiber: 3g / sodium: 3mg*

Vanilla-Poached Apricots

Prep time: 10 minutes   Cook time: 1 minute   Serves 6

- 1¼ cups water
- ¼ cup marsala wine
- ¼ cup sugar
- 1 teaspoon vanilla bean paste
- 8 medium apricots, sliced in half and pitted

1. Place all ingredients in the Instant Pot®. Stir to combine. Close lid, set steam release to Sealing, press the Manual button, and set time to 1 minute.
2. When the timer beeps, quick-release the pressure until the float valve drops. Press the Cancel button and open the lid. Let stand for 10 minutes. Carefully remove apricots from poaching liquid with a slotted spoon. Serve warm or at room temperature.

Per Serving:*calories: 62 / fat: 0g / protein: 2g / carbs: 14g / fiber: 1g / sodium: 10mg*

Peaches Poached in Rose Water

Prep time: 15 minutes   Cook time: 1 minute   Serves 6

- 1 cup water
- 1 cup rose water
- ¼ cup wildflower honey
- 8 green cardamom pods, lightly crushed
- 1 teaspoon vanilla bean paste
- 6 large yellow peaches, pitted and quartered
- ½ cup chopped unsalted roasted pistachio meats

1. Add water, rose water, honey, cardamom, and vanilla to the Instant Pot®. Whisk well, then add peaches. Close lid, set steam release to Sealing, press the Manual button, and set time to 1 minute.
2. When the timer beeps, quick-release the pressure until the float valve drops. Press the Cancel button and open lid. Allow peaches to stand for 10 minutes. Carefully remove peaches from poaching liquid with a slotted spoon.
3. Slip skins from peach slices. Arrange slices on a plate and garnish with pistachios. Serve warm or at room temperature.

Per Serving:calories: 145 / fat: 3g / protein: 2g / carbs: 28g / fiber: 2g / sodium: 8mg

Poached Apricots and Pistachios with Greek Yogurt

Prep time: 2 minutes   Cook time: 18 minutes   Serves 4

- ½ cup orange juice
- 2 tablespoons brandy
- 2 tablespoons honey
- ¾ cup water
- 1 cinnamon stick
- 12 dried apricots
- ⅓ cup 2% Greek yogurt
- 2 tablespoons mascarpone cheese
- 2 tablespoons shelled pistachios

1. Place a saucepan over medium heat and add the orange juice, brandy, honey, and water. Stir to combine, then add the cinnamon stick.
2. Once the honey has dissolved, add the apricots. Bring the mixture to a boil, then cover, reduce the heat to low, and simmer for 15 minutes.
3. While the apricots are simmering, combine the Greek yogurt and mascarpone cheese in a small serving bowl. Stir until smooth, then set aside.
4. When the cooking time for the apricots is complete, uncover, add the pistachios, and continue simmering for 3 more minutes. Remove the pan from the heat.
5. To serve, divide the Greek yogurt–mascarpone cheese mixture into 4 serving bowls and top each serving with 3 apricots, a few pistachios, and 1 teaspoon of the syrup. The apricots and syrup can be stored in a jar at room temperature for up to 1 month.

Per Serving:calories: 146 / fat: 3g / protein: 4g / carbs: 28g / fiber: 4g / sodium: 62mg

10

Salads

Arugula and Artichokes

Prep time: 20 minutes   Cook time: 0 minutes   Serves 6

- 4 tablespoons olive oil
- 2 tablespoons balsamic vinegar
- 1 teaspoon Dijon mustard
- 1 clove garlic, minced
- 6 cups baby arugula leaves
- 6 oil-packed artichoke hearts, sliced
- 6 low-salt olives, pitted and chopped
- 1 cup cherry tomatoes, sliced in half
- 4 fresh basil leaves, thinly sliced

1. Make the dressing by whisking together the olive oil, vinegar, Dijon, and garlic until you have a smooth emulsion. Set aside.
2. Toss the arugula, artichokes, olives, and tomatoes together.
3. Drizzle the salad with the dressing, garnish with the fresh basil, and serve.

Per Serving:calories: 133 / fat: 12g / protein: 2g / carbs: 6g / fiber: 3g / sodium: 75mg

Roasted Broccoli Panzanella Salad

Prep time: 10 minutes   Cook time: 20 minutes   Serves: 4

- 1 pound (454 g) broccoli (about 3 medium stalks), trimmed, cut into 1-inch florets and ½-inch stem slices
- 3 tablespoons extra-virgin olive oil, divided
- 1 pint cherry or grape tomatoes (about 1½ cups)
- 1½ teaspoons honey, divided
- 3 cups cubed whole-grain crusty bread
- 1 tablespoon balsamic vinegar
- ½ teaspoon freshly ground black pepper
- ¼ teaspoon kosher or sea salt
- Grated Parmesan cheese (or other hard cheese) and chopped fresh oregano leaves, for serving (optional)

1. Place a large, rimmed baking sheet in the oven. Preheat the oven to 450°F(235°C) with the pan inside.
2. Put the broccoli in a large bowl, and drizzle with 1 tablespoon of the oil. Toss to coat.
3. Carefully remove the hot baking sheet from the oven and spoon the broccoli onto it, leaving some oil in the bottom of the bowl. Add the tomatoes to the same bowl, and toss to coat with the leftover oil (don't add any more oil). Toss the tomatoes with 1 teaspoon of honey, and scrape them onto the baking sheet with the broccoli.
4. Roast for 15 minutes, stirring halfway through. Remove the sheet from the oven, and add the bread cubes. Roast for 3 more minutes. The broccoli is ready when it appears slightly charred on the tips and is tender-crisp when poked with a fork.
5. Spoon the vegetable mixture onto a serving plate or into a large, flat bowl.
6. In a small bowl, whisk the remaining 2 tablespoons of oil together with the vinegar, the remaining ½ teaspoon of honey, and the pepper and salt. Pour over the salad, and toss gently. Sprinkle with cheese and oregano, if desired, and serve.

Per Serving:calories: 197 / fat: 12g / protein: 7g / carbs: 19g / fiber: 5g / sodium: 296mg

Cauliflower Tabbouleh Salad

Prep time: 15 minutes | Cook time: 0 minutes | Serves 4

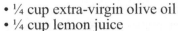

- ¼ cup extra-virgin olive oil
- ¼ cup lemon juice
- Zest of 1 lemon
- ¾ teaspoon kosher salt
- ½ teaspoon ground turmeric
- ¼ teaspoon ground coriander
- ¼ teaspoon ground cumin
- ¼ teaspoon black pepper
- ⅛ teaspoon ground cinnamon
- 1 pound (454 g) riced cauliflower
- 1 English cucumber, diced
- 12 cherry tomatoes, halved
- 1 cup fresh parsley, chopped
- ½ cup fresh mint, chopped

1. In a large bowl, whisk together the olive oil, lemon juice, lemon zest, salt, turmeric, coriander, cumin, black pepper, and cinnamon.
2. Add the riced cauliflower to the bowl and mix well. Add in the cucumber, tomatoes, parsley, and mint and gently mix together.

Per Serving:calories: 180 / fat: 15g / protein: 4g / carbs: 12g / fiber: 5g / sodium:260 mg

Israeli Salad with Nuts and Seeds

Prep time: 15 minutes | Cook time: 0 minutes | Serves 4

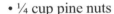

- ¼ cup pine nuts
- ¼ cup shelled pistachios
- ¼ cup coarsely chopped walnuts
- ¼ cup shelled pumpkin seeds
- ¼ cup shelled sunflower seeds
- 2 large English cucumbers, unpeeled and finely chopped
- 1 pint cherry tomatoes, finely chopped
- ½ small red onion, finely chopped
- ½ cup finely chopped fresh flat-leaf Italian parsley
- ¼ cup extra-virgin olive oil
- 2 to 3 tablespoons freshly squeezed lemon juice (from 1 lemon)
- 1 teaspoon salt
- ¼ teaspoon freshly ground black pepper
- 4 cups baby arugula

1. In a large dry skillet, toast the pine nuts, pistachios, walnuts, pumpkin seeds, and sunflower seeds over medium-low heat until golden and fragrant, 5 to 6 minutes, being careful not to burn them. Remove from the heat and set aside.
2. In a large bowl, combine the cucumber, tomatoes, red onion, and parsley.
3. In a small bowl, whisk together olive oil, lemon juice, salt, and pepper. Pour over the chopped vegetables and toss to coat.
4. Add the toasted nuts and seeds and arugula and toss with the salad to blend well. Serve at room temperature or chilled.

Per Serving:calories: 404 / fat: 36g / protein: 10g / carbs: 16g / fiber: 5g / sodium: 601mg

Flank Steak Spinach Salad

Prep time: 15 minutes   Cook time: 10 minutes   Serves 4

- 1 pound (454 g) flank steak
- 1 teaspoon extra-virgin olive oil
- 1 tablespoon garlic powder
- ½ teaspoon salt
- ½ teaspoon freshly ground black pepper
- 4 cups baby spinach leaves
- 10 cherry tomatoes, halved
- 10 cremini or white mushrooms, sliced
- 1 small red onion, thinly sliced
- ½ red bell pepper, thinly sliced

1. Preheat the broiler. Line a baking sheet with aluminum foil.
2. Rub the top of the flank steak with the olive oil, garlic powder, salt, and pepper and let sit for 10 minutes before placing under the broiler. Broil for 5 minutes on each side for medium rare. Allow the meat to rest on a cutting board for 10 minutes.
3. Meanwhile, in a large bowl, combine the spinach, tomatoes, mushrooms, onion, and bell pepper and toss well.
4. To serve, divide the salad among 4 dinner plates. Slice the steak on the diagonal and place 4 to 5 slices on top of each salad. Serve with your favorite vinaigrette.

Per Serving:calories: 211 / fat: 7g / protein: 28g / carbs: 9g / fiber: 2g / sodium: 382mg

Yellow and White Hearts of Palm Salad

Prep time: 10 minutes   Cook time: 0 minutes   Serves 4

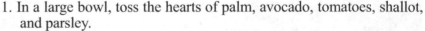

- 2 (14-ounce / 397-g) cans hearts of palm, drained and cut into ½-inch-thick slices
- 1 avocado, cut into ½-inch pieces
- 1 cup halved yellow cherry tomatoes
- ½ small shallot, thinly sliced
- ¼ cup coarsely chopped flat-leaf parsley
- 2 tablespoons low-fat mayonnaise
- 2 tablespoons extra-virgin olive oil
- ¼ teaspoon salt
- ⅛ teaspoon freshly ground black pepper

1. In a large bowl, toss the hearts of palm, avocado, tomatoes, shallot, and parsley.
2. In a small bowl, whisk the mayonnaise, olive oil, salt, and pepper, then mix into the large bowl.

Per Serving:calories: 192 / fat: 15g / protein: 5g / carbs: 14g / fiber: 7g / sodium: 841mg

Cabbage and Carrot Salad

Prep time: 10 minutes   Cook time: 0 minutes   Serves 3

- ½ medium head cabbage, thinly sliced, rinsed, and drained
- 3 medium carrots, peeled and shredded
- 4 tablespoons extra virgin olive oil
- 3 tablespoons fresh lemon juice
- ½ teaspoon salt
- ¼ teaspoon freshly ground black pepper
- 1 garlic clove, minced
- 8 Kalamata olives, pitted

1. Place the cabbage and carrots in a large bowl and toss.
2. In a jar or small bowl, combine the olive oil, lemon juice, salt, black pepper, and garlic. Whisk or shake to combine.
3. Pour the dressing over the salad and toss. (Note that it will reduce in volume.) 4. Scatter the olives over the salad just before serving. Store covered in the refrigerator for up to 2 days.

Per Serving:calories: 237 / fat: 19g / protein: 3g / carbs: 16g / fiber: 6g / sodium: 570mg

Classic Tabouli

Prep time: 30 minutes   Cook time: 0 minutes   Serves 8 to 10

- 1 cup bulgur wheat, grind
- 4 cups Italian parsley, finely chopped
- 2 cups ripe tomato, finely diced
- 1 cup green onion, finely chopped
- ½ cup lemon juice
- ½ cup extra-virgin olive oil
- 1½ teaspoons salt
- 1 teaspoon dried mint

1. Before you chop the vegetables, put the bulgur in a small bowl. Rinse with water, drain, and let stand in the bowl while you prepare the other ingredients.
2. Put the parsley, tomatoes, green onion, and bulgur into a large bowl.
3. In a small bowl, whisk together the lemon juice, olive oil, salt, and mint.
4. Pour the dressing over the tomato, onion, and bulgur mixture, tossing everything together. Add additional salt to taste. Serve immediately or store in the fridge for up to 2 days.

Per Serving:calories: 207 / fat: 14g / protein: 4g / carbs: 20g / fiber: 5g / sodium: 462mg

Pizzas, Wraps, and Sandwiches

Greek Salad Wraps

Prep time: 15 minutes Cook time: 0 minutes Serves: 4

- 1½ cups seedless cucumber, peeled and chopped (about 1 large cucumber)
- 1 cup chopped tomato (about 1 large tomato)
- ½ cup finely chopped fresh mint
- 1 (2¼ ounces / 64 g) can sliced black olives (about ½ cup), drained
- ¼ cup diced red onion (about ¼ onion)
- 2 tablespoons extra-virgin olive oil
- 1 tablespoon red wine vinegar
- ¼ teaspoon freshly ground black pepper
- ¼ teaspoon kosher or sea salt
- ½ cup crumbled goat cheese (about 2 ounces / 57 g)
- 4 whole-wheat flatbread wraps or soft whole-wheat tortillas

1. In a large bowl, mix together the cucumber, tomato, mint, olives, and onion until well combined.
2. In a small bowl, whisk together the oil, vinegar, pepper, and salt. Drizzle the dressing over the salad, and mix gently.
3. With a knife, spread the goat cheese evenly over the four wraps. Spoon a quarter of the salad filling down the middle of each wrap.
4. Fold up each wrap: Start by folding up the bottom, then fold one side over and fold the other side over the top. Repeat with the remaining wraps and serve.

Per Serving:calories: 217 / fat: 14g / protein: 7g / carbs: 17g / fiber: 3g / sodium: 329mg

Pesto Chicken Mini Pizzas

Prep time: 5 minutes Cook time: 10 minutes Serves 4

- 2 cups shredded cooked chicken
- ¾ cup pesto
- 4 English muffins, split
- 2 cups shredded Mozzarella cheese

1. In a medium bowl, toss the chicken with the pesto. Place one-eighth of the chicken on each English muffin half. Top each English muffin with ¼ cup of the Mozzarella cheese.
2. Put four pizzas at a time in the air fryer and air fry at 350°F (177°C) for 5 minutes. Repeat this process with the other four pizzas.

Per Serving:calories: 617 / fat: 36g / protein: 45g / carbs: 29g / fiber: 3g / sodium: 544mg

Margherita Open-Face Sandwiches

Prep time: 10 minutes | Cook time: 5 minutes | Serves: 4

- 2 (6- to 7-inch) whole-wheat submarine or hoagie rolls, sliced open horizontally
- 1 tablespoon extra-virgin olive oil
- 1 garlic clove, halved
- 1 large ripe tomato, cut into 8 slices
- ¼ teaspoon dried oregano
- 1 cup fresh mozzarella (about 4 ounces / 113 g), patted dry and sliced
- ¼ cup lightly packed fresh basil leaves, torn into small pieces
- ¼ teaspoon freshly ground black pepper

1. Preheat the broiler to high with the rack 4 inches under the heating element.
2. Place the sliced bread on a large, rimmed baking sheet. Place under the broiler for 1 minute, until the bread is just lightly toasted. Remove from the oven.
3. Brush each piece of the toasted bread with the oil, and rub a garlic half over each piece.
4. Place the toasted bread back on the baking sheet. Evenly distribute the tomato slices on each piece, sprinkle with the oregano, and layer the cheese on top.
5. Place the baking sheet under the broiler. Set the timer for 1½ minutes, but check after 1 minute. When the cheese is melted and the edges are just starting to get dark brown, remove the sandwiches from the oven (this can take anywhere from 1½ to 2 minutes).
6. Top each sandwich with the fresh basil and pepper.

Per Serving:calories: 176 / fat: 9g / protein: 10g / carbs: 14g / fiber: 2g / sodium: 119mg

Cucumber Basil Sandwiches

Prep time: 10 minutes | Cook time: 0 minutes | Serves 2

- Cucumber Basil Sandwiches
- 4 slices whole-grain bread
- ¼ cup hummus
- 1 large cucumber, thinly sliced
- 4 whole basil leaves

1. Spread the hummus on 2 slices of bread, and layer the cucumbers onto it. Top with the basil leaves and close the sandwiches.
2. Press down lightly and serve immediately.

Per Serving:calories: 209 / fat: 5g / protein: 9g / carbs: 32g / fiber: 6g / sodium: 275mg

Turkish Pizza

Prep time: 20 minutes   Cook time: 10 minutes   Serves 4

- 4 ounces (113 g) ground lamb or 85% lean ground beef
- ¼ cup finely chopped green bell pepper
- ¼ cup chopped fresh parsley
- 1 small plum tomato, seeded and finely chopped
- 2 tablespoons finely chopped yellow onion
- 1 garlic clove, minced   • 2 teaspoons tomato paste
- ¼ teaspoon sweet paprika   • ¼ teaspoon ground cumin
- ⅛ to ¼ teaspoon red pepper flakes
- ⅛ teaspoon ground allspice
- ⅛ teaspoon kosher salt
- ⅛ teaspoon black pepper
- 4 (6-inch) flour tortillas
- For Serving:
- Chopped fresh mint
- Extra-virgin olive oil
- Lemon wedges

1. In a medium bowl, gently mix the ground lamb, bell pepper, parsley, chopped tomato, onion, garlic, tomato paste, paprika, cumin, red pepper flakes, allspice, salt, and black pepper until well combined.
2. Divide the meat mixture evenly among the tortillas, spreading it all the way to the edge of each tortilla.
3. Place 1 tortilla in the air fryer basket. Set the air fryer to 400°F (204°C) for 10 minutes, or until the meat topping has browned and the edge of the tortilla is golden. Transfer to a plate and repeat to cook the remaining tortillas.
4. Serve the pizzas warm, topped with chopped fresh mint and a drizzle of extra-virgin olive oil and with lemon wedges alongside.

Per Serving:calories: 172 / fat: 8g / protein: 8g / carbs: 18g / fiber: 2g / sodium: 318mg

Chicken and Goat Cheese Pizza

Prep time: 10 minutes   Cook time: 10 minutes   Serves 4

- All-purpose flour, for dusting
- 1 pound (454 g) premade pizza dough
- 2 tablespoons olive oil
- 1 cup shredded cooked chicken
- 3 ounces (85 g) goat cheese, crumbled
- Sea salt
- Freshly ground black pepper

1. Preheat the oven to 475°F (245°C).
2. On a floured surface, roll out the dough to a 12-inch round and place it on a lightly floured pizza pan or baking sheet. Drizzle the dough with the olive oil and spread it out evenly. Top the dough with the chicken and goat cheese.
3. Bake the pizza for 8 to 10 minutes, until the crust is cooked through and golden.
4. Season with salt and pepper and serve.

Per Serving:calories: 555 / fat: 23g / protein: 24g / carbs: 60g / fiber: 2g / sodium: 660mg

Dill Salmon Salad Wraps

Prep time: 10 minutes   Cook time: 10 minutes   Serves:6

- 1 pound (454 g) salmon filet, cooked and flaked, or 3 (5-ounce / 142-g) cans salmon
- ½ cup diced carrots (about 1 carrot)
- ½ cup diced celery (about 1 celery stalk)
- 3 tablespoons chopped fresh dill
- 3 tablespoons diced red onion (a little less than ⅛ onion)
- 2 tablespoons capers
- 1½ tablespoons extra-virgin olive oil
- 1 tablespoon aged balsamic vinegar
- ½ teaspoon freshly ground black pepper
- ¼ teaspoon kosher or sea salt
- 4 whole-wheat flatbread wraps or soft whole-wheat tortillas

1. In a large bowl, mix together the salmon, carrots, celery, dill, red onion, capers, oil, vinegar, pepper, and salt.
2. Divide the salmon salad among the flatbreads. Fold up the bottom of the flatbread, then roll up the wrap and serve.

Per Serving:calories: 185 / fat: 8g / protein: 17g / carbs: 12g / fiber: 2g / sodium: 237mg

Grilled Chicken Salad Pita

Prep time: 15 minutes   Cook time: 16 minutes   Serves 1

- 1 boneless, skinless chicken breast
- Sea salt and freshly ground pepper, to taste
- 1 cup baby spinach
- 1 roasted red pepper, sliced
- 1 tomato, chopped
- ½ small red onion, thinly sliced
- ½ small cucumber, chopped
- 1 tablespoon olive oil
- Juice of 1 lemon
- 1 whole-wheat pita pocket
- 2 tablespoons crumbled feta cheese

1. Preheat a gas or charcoal grill to medium-high heat.
2. Season the chicken breast with sea salt and freshly ground pepper, and grill until cooked through, about 7–8 minutes per side.
3. Allow chicken to rest for 5 minutes before slicing into strips.
4. While the chicken is cooking, put all the chopped vegetables into a medium-mixing bowl and season with sea salt and freshly ground pepper.
5. Chop the chicken into cubes and add to salad. Add the olive oil and lemon juice and toss well.
6. Stuff the mixture onto a pita pocket and top with the feta cheese. Serve immediately.

Per Serving:calories: 653 / fat: 26g / protein: 71g / carbs: 34g / fiber: 6g / sodium: 464mg

Classic Margherita Pizza

Prep time: 10 minutes   Cook time: 10 minutes   Serves 4

- All-purpose flour, for dusting • 1 pound (454 g) premade pizza dough
- 1 (15-ounce / 425-g) can crushed San Marzano tomatoes, with their juices
- 2 garlic cloves   • 1 teaspoon Italian seasoning
- Pinch sea salt, plus more as needed
- 1½ teaspoons olive oil, for drizzling
- 10 slices mozzarella cheese   • 12 to 15 fresh basil leaves

1. Preheat the oven to 475ºF (245ºC).
2. On a floured surface, roll out the dough to a 12-inch round and place it on a lightly floured pizza pan or baking sheet.
3. In a food processor, combine the tomatoes with their juices, garlic, Italian seasoning, and salt and process until smooth. Taste and adjust the seasoning.
4. Drizzle the olive oil over the pizza dough, then spoon the pizza sauce over the dough and spread it out evenly with the back of the spoon, leaving a 1-inch border. Evenly distribute the mozzarella over the pizza.
5. Bake until the crust is cooked through and golden, 8 to 10 minutes. Remove from the oven and let sit for 1 to 2 minutes. Top with the basil right before serving.

Per Serving: calories: 570 / fat: 21g / protein: 28g / carbs: 66g / fiber: 4g / sodium: 570mg

Bocadillo with Herbed Tuna and Piquillo Peppers

Prep time: 5 minutes   Cook time: 20 minutes   Serves 4

- 2 tablespoons olive oil, plus more for brushing
- 1 medium onion, finely chopped
- 2 leeks, white and tender green parts only, finely chopped
- 1 teaspoon chopped thyme   • ½ teaspoon dried marjoram
- ½ teaspoon salt
- ¼ teaspoon freshly ground black pepper
- 3 tablespoons sherry vinegar • 1 carrot, finely diced
- 2 (8-ounce / 227-g) jars Spanish tuna in olive oil
- 4 crusty whole-wheat sandwich rolls, split
- 1 ripe tomato, grated on the large holes of a box grater
- 4 piquillo peppers, cut into thin strips

1. Heat 2 tablespoons of olive oil in a medium skillet over medium heat. Add the onion, leeks, thyme, marjoram, salt, and pepper. Stir frequently until the onions are softened, about 10 minutes. Stir in the vinegar and carrot and cook until the liquid has evaporated, 5 minutes. Transfer the mixture to a bowl and let cool to room temperature or refrigerate for 15 minutes or so.
2. In a medium bowl, combine the tuna, along with its oil, with the onion mixture, breaking the tuna chunks up with a fork.
3. Brush the rolls lightly with oil and toast under the broiler until lightly browned, about 2 minutes. Spoon the tomato pulp onto the bottom half of each roll, dividing equally and spreading it with the back of the spoon. Divide the tuna mixture among the rolls and top with the piquillo pepper slices. Serve immediately.

Per Serving: calories: 416 / fat: 18g / protein: 35g / carbs: 30g / fiber: 5g / sodium: 520mg

6-Week Meal Plan

	Breakfast	Lunch	Dinner	Snack/Dessert
Monday	Greek Yogurt Parfait with Granola	Easy Honey-Garlic Pork Chops	Sweet Potato and Chickpea Moroccan Stew	Slow-Cooked Fruit Medley
Tuesday	Summer Day Fruit Salad	Chickpeas with Spinach and Sun-Dried Tomatoes	Rack of Lamb with Pistachio Crust	Avocado-Orange Fruit Salad
Wednesdays	Tiropita (Greek Cheese Pie)	Greek Lamb Burgers	Roasted Broccoli Panzanella Salad	Fresh Figs with Chocolate Sauce
Thursdays	Jalapeño Popper Egg Cups	Beef Burger	Earthy Lentil and Rice Pilaf	Vanilla-Poached Apricots
Fridays	Berry Warming Smoothie	Lebanese Grilled Chicken	Skinny Fries	Poached Apricots and Pistachios with Greek Yogurt
Saturdays	Lemon–Olive Oil Breakfast Cakes with Berry Syrup	Chickpea Fritters	Arugula and Artichokes	Peaches Poached in Rose Water
Sunday	Quinoa and Yogurt Breakfast Bowls	Cheese-Stuffed Dates	Cube Steak Roll-Ups	Slow-Cooked Fruit Medley
Monday	Garden Scramble	Pork and Cannellini Bean Stew	Quinoa with Kale, Carrots, and Walnuts	Avocado-Orange Fruit Salad
Tuesday	Spanish Tortilla with Potatoes and Peppers	Fried Zucchini Salad	Chicken Cacciatore	Fresh Figs with Chocolate Sauce
Wednesdays	Greek Breakfast Power Bowl	Moroccan Date Pilaf	Cauliflower Tabbouleh Salad	Vanilla-Poached Apricots
Thursdays	Egg Baked in Avocado	Cheesy Dates	Mustard Lamb Chops	Poached Apricots and Pistachios with Greek Yogurt
Fridays	Peach Sunrise Smoothie	Falafel	Margherita Open-Face Sandwiches	Peaches Poached in Rose Water
Saturdays	Greek Yogurt Parfait with Granola	Hearty Stewed Beef in Tomato Sauce	Shrimp over Black Bean Linguine	Slow-Cooked Fruit Medley
Sunday	Summer Day Fruit Salad	Herb–Marinated Chicken Breasts	Turkish Pizza	Avocado-Orange Fruit Salad

	Breakfast	Lunch	Dinner	Snack/Dessert
Monday	Tiropita (Greek Cheese Pie)	Bulgur and Beef–Stuffed Peppers	Earthy Whole Brown Lentil Dhal	Fresh Figs with Chocolate Sauce
Tuesday	Jalapeño Popper Egg Cups	Stuffed Artichokes	Greek Salad Wraps	Vanilla-Poached Apricots
Wednesdays	Berry Warming Smoothie	Israeli Salad with Nuts and Seeds	Filipino Crispy Pork Belly	Poached Apricots and Pistachios with Greek Yogurt
Thursdays	Lemon–Olive Oil Breakfast Cakes with Berry Syrup	Ground Beef Taco Rolls	Fava Bean Purée with Chicory	Peaches Poached in Rose Water
Fridays	Quinoa and Yogurt Breakfast Bowls	Chicken with Lemon Asparagus	Classic Tabouli	Slow-Cooked Fruit Medley
Saturdays	Garden Scramble	Flank Steak Spinach Salad	Spaghetti Zoodles and Meatballs	Avocado-Orange Fruit Salad
Sunday	Spanish Tortilla with Potatoes and Peppers	Personal Cauliflower Pizzas	Yellow and White Hearts of Palm Salad	Fresh Figs with Chocolate Sauce
Monday	Greek Breakfast Power Bowl	Crustless Spinach Cheese Pie	Turmeric-Spiced Crunchy Chickpeas	Vanilla-Poached Apricots
Tuesday	Egg Baked in Avocado	Blackened Cajun Chicken Tenders	Cabbage and Carrot Salad	Poached Apricots and Pistachios with Greek Yogurt
Wednesdays	Peach Sunrise Smoothie	Tortellini in Red Pepper Sauce	Grape Chicken Panzanella	Peaches Poached in Rose Water
Thursdays	Greek Yogurt Parfait with Granola	Pecan Turkey Cutlets	Caprese Eggplant Stacks	Slow-Cooked Fruit Medley
Fridays	Summer Day Fruit Salad	Vegetable Pot Stickers	Pecan Turkey Cutlets	Avocado-Orange Fruit Salad
Saturdays	Tiropita (Greek Cheese Pie)	Spinach and Sweet Pepper Poppers	Citrus-Marinated Olives	Fresh Figs with Chocolate Sauce
Sunday	Jalapeño Popper Egg Cups	Skillet Greek Turkey and Rice	Roasted Veggie Bowl	Vanilla-Poached Apricots
Monday	Berry Warming Smoothie	Tuna Nuggets in Hoisin Sauce	Southern Italian Seafood Stew in Tomato Broth	Poached Apricots and Pistachios with Greek Yogurt

	Breakfast	Lunch	Dinner	Snack/Dessert
Tuesday	Lemon–Olive Oil Breakfast Cakes with Berry Syrup	Greek Garlic Dip	Crustless Spanakopita	Peaches Poached in Rose Water
Wednesdays	Quinoa and Yogurt Breakfast Bowls	Niçoise Chicken	Burrata Caprese Stack	Slow-Cooked Fruit Medley
Thursdays	Garden Scramble	Potato Vegetable Hash	South Indian Fried Fish	Avocado-Orange Fruit Salad
Fridays	Spanish Tortilla with Potatoes and Peppers	Mediterranean Roasted Turkey Breast	Freekeh, Chickpea, and Herb Salad	Fresh Figs with Chocolate Sauce
Saturdays	Greek Breakfast Power Bowl	Lemon-Thyme Asparagus	Rosemary Salmon	Vanilla-Poached Apricots
Sunday	Egg Baked in Avocado	Italian Crepe with Herbs and Onion	Taco-Spiced Chickpeas	Poached Apricots and Pistachios with Greek Yogurt
Monday	Peach Sunrise Smoothie	Chicken and Grape Tomatoes	Three-Cheese Zucchini Boats	Peaches Poached in Rose Water
Tuesday	Jalapeño Popper Egg Cups	Stuffed Fried Mushrooms	Lemon and Herb Fish Packets	Slow-Cooked Fruit Medley
Wednesdays	Garden Scramble	Greek Bean Soup	Moroccan Crusted Sea Bass	Avocado-Orange Fruit Salad
Thursdays	Quinoa and Yogurt Breakfast Bowls	Fish Tagine	Honey and Spice Glazed Carrots	Fresh Figs with Chocolate Sauce
Fridays	Greek Breakfast Power Bowl	Stuffed Fried Mushrooms	Almond-Encrusted Salmon	Vanilla-Poached Apricots
Saturdays	Summer Day Fruit Salad	Mixed Seafood Soup	Baked Turkey Kibbeh	Poached Apricots and Pistachios with Greek Yogurt
Sunday	Greek Yogurt Parfait with Granola	Honeyed Salmon	Rice Pilaf with Dill	Peaches Poached in Rose Water

INDEX

Made in the USA
Las Vegas, NV
22 June 2024

91356467R00046